A Heart FOR Nepal

The Dr. Helen Huston Story

Dr. Huston interviewing a patient at Amp Pipal.

A Heart FOR Nepal
The Dr. Helen Huston Story

Gerald W. Hankins

Windflower Communications

Winnipeg, Manitoba, Canada

Published by Windflower Communications, Winnipeg, Manitoba.

Canadian Cataloguing in Publication Data

Hankins, Gerald W.
  A heart for Nepal
  ISBN 1-895308-09-7
1. Huston, Helen. 2. Missionaries, Medical - Nepal - Biography.
3. United Church of Canada - Missions - Nepal. I. Title.

R722.32.H87H35 1992 266'.0092 C92-098183-6

Cover art and design by Kathryn Dahl, Winnipeg, MB
Line drawings by Lisa Jansen, Calgary, AB
Printed in Canada by Derksen Printers, Steinbach, MB

International Standard Book Number: 1-895308-09-7

Introduction

Dr. Helen Huston is one of my personal heroines. Hers is the kind of life of dedication and action which I, a sedentary, cautious sort myself, most admire. I had already known of the work of this dedicated woman before I moved from Edmonton to our farm home in east-central Alberta. In the area into which I moved, I found that she was not just a legend, but a person known and loved. She had spoken in many churches in the area, and had been camp doctor and guest speaker at Camp Whitney, the United Church camp just a few miles north of where I live. Frequently I met and talked with people whose lives and attitudes had been affected permanently by their association with her.

I have still met Dr. Helen Huston only through the reports of those who know her. Therefore, I have looked forward to the publication of this work. Thanks to the dedication of her colleague, Dr. Gerry Hankins, the formidable task of telling an impressive life story while it is still being lived has been accomplished. I celebrate having a chance to know more about this internationally respected woman.

Helen Huston's life of dedicated service to humanity through the little hospital in the hills of Amp Pipal, Nepal has been recognized with many honours, including the University of Alberta's Medical Alumni Achievement Award (1978) and the Sir Edmund Hillary Foundation Award for Humanitarian Service (1991). In 1984, an honorary doctorate was conferred upon her by the University of Alberta.

Addressing Convocation on that occassion, she issued an urgent and emotional appeal to the students of her own *alma mater* to live as members of one human family, "made of the same clay." Congratulating them on their achievements, she asked them with what I understand to be a characteristic directness: "Will you . . . choose *money*? Things, security, pleasure, power, prestige? Or will you seek for the Potter's plan and purpose for your life?"

This book will encourage us all to consider the challenge not only of her words, but of her life.

—Maxine Hancock, Ph. D.

Preface

Not every would-be writer of the biography of a distinguished person has the opportunity to draw upon a long acquaintanceship, let alone a friendship.

The author here considers himself very fortunate in this respect. Helen Huston and I were classmates in medical school at the University of Alberta (Helen somewhat closer to the top of the class than I). Then in 1974 my wife Alison and I, along with our daughter Jennifer, joined the United Mission to Nepal where Helen had already been serving for fourteen years.

In spite of working at different locations in Nepal, we met Helen periodically and friendship grew. Short periods working with Helen at Amp Pipal hospital enabled us to know her better.

We resigned from the Mission in 1986 and returned to Canada. But two years before leaving Nepal, the seed of an idea had been sown, and seemed to want to sprout. What about writing Helen's life story? As an outstanding and devoted medical missionary who pioneered the founding of a hospital in the hills of Nepal, her life seemed to merit a permanent record. And circumstances were such that I appeared to have the qualifications to do it.

Now the job has been completed. Just to be able to study and then write about the exciting life of this great lady has been for me the privilege of a lifetime.

It is my delight to share the record of her career with you, the reader.

Acknowledgements

Many people have helped the author write this book.

I especially wish to thank Theresa White for her great help in editing and typing. Her work was invaluable. Theresa even managed a quick trip to Nepal "to see for herself." Thanks also for the assistance of her husband, Lorne. Their friend, Myrt Johnson, gave much help with the typing.

Helen's family and friends, scattered world-wide, sent me letters, tapes, clippings and pictures—for all these I am grateful.

By his encouragement and example, Dr. Tom Hale, a former UMNer, showed me that surgeons can do more than make incisions!

Thanks to Byron Christopher of CBC, Edmonton, for the use of his fine picture of Helen and the Gurung lady on page (i).

The superb line drawings of Lisa Jansen have been a wonderful contribution. Lisa, daughter of Jim Miller who built most of the Amp Pipal hospital, created them during eight-month-old Austin's nap time.

Gilbert Brandt of Windflower Communications has been most patient and understanding.

From the beginning, my wife Alison and our children, all of whom have met Helen, have encouraged the writing of this book.

A more cooperative subject than Helen Huston would be hard to find, in spite of her natural dislike of the limelight. She shared with me hundreds of personal letters and many hours of delightful interview-time.

For the practical help and support of these and unnamed others, I am most grateful.

Contents

1

The Most Precious Things of Life

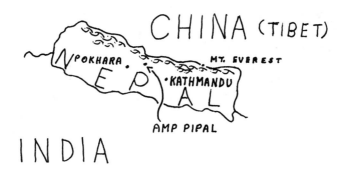

On November 21, 1991 several hundred guests assembled at the Sutton Place Hotel, Toronto, Canada for a gala "black tie" dinner.

The evening's program reached a climax when a tall man with bushy, grey temples and attired in a black dress suit arose from his place at the centre of the head table. A few seconds later a lady, also tall and greying and dressed in a red and emerald green Indian silk sari, stood up beside him. They shook hands and tried to speak but handclapping and cheering blotted out any words they tried to share.

The man was Sir Edmund Hillary, world-renowned mountaineer and explorer. A native of New Zealand, he and Tensing Norquay had climbed Mt. Everest on May 29, 1953, the first humans to reach the summit of earth's highest mountain. Not long after Everest, he set up

1

the Hillary Foundation to provide schools and medical facilities in Nepal in gratitude to the Sherpa people. Their part in that "first ascent" had been vital, he said.

Beside Sir Hillary stood Dr. Helen Huston, tall and straight. A Canadian missionary doctor, she had devoted nearly all her adult life to the people of Nepal. Recognizing her long and outstanding contribution, the Hillary Foundation had flown her back to Canada to be the first person to receive its Award for Humanitarian Service.

Sir Hillary made the presentation, citing "her dedicated commitment to the improvement of the quality of life for the people of the Himalayan regions of Nepal."

"Things have changed a little since our first ascent in 1953," said Sir Hillary, noting the great advances in technology. "Last year my son Peter stood on the summit of Everest and placed a long distance phone call to me in Auckland."

Things had changed too in the hilly and primitive Gorkha District of Nepal where Dr. Helen had served for almost thirty-one years. But in her address she said little about her own pioneering efforts as a doctor and founder of a hospital seven hours' walk from any road.

Lady June Hillary, Sir Edmund Hillary, Mrs. Ang Ang Mu Sherpa, Mr. Ang Rita Sherpa (from Nepal), Dr. Helen Huston (with award).

"There are thousands of people serving in remote places of the world who should be getting the award more than I, but I am pleased to accept it on behalf of them."

She went on to speak about Sir Hillary's contributions to Nepal and to say "how wonderful it is to be here with so many people who love Nepal and the Nepali people."

Before sitting down, she summed up her philosophy of missions and the goal of her work in Nepal. "So let's go on loving Nepalis, teaching them, sharing the most precious things of life with them, and working ourselves out of a job."

Dr. Helen then expressed thanks for the Award—as she had done for the many other honours that had come her way—but her heart was really back in the little village of Amp Pipal in the hills of Nepal.

2

Crisis at Amp Pipal

It was early morning, and I was starting up the ramp toward the operating room when I heard an urgent call behind me. I wheeled around and ran back down the dark stone-walled corridor.

Amp Pipal Hospital in the hills of Nepal wasn't the kind of environment most Canadian doctors would be used to working in, but by this time, in March, 1986, I had learned to take its peculiarities in stride. I narrowly avoided tripping over a cleaner who was scrubbing the cement floor as I turned quickly into the intensive care unit. There was no state-of-the-art medical equipment here. In fact, the only thing that set this room apart as "intensive" was its nearness to the nurses' station.

Four or five people rose from benches surrounding a small cot as I entered the room to join the doctor who had called for my help. I fixed my attention immediately on the boy stretched out on the cot, his right arm in a plaster cast. Sweat trickled down his forehead into his dark, sunken eyes. He breathed heavily, jerkily. The muscles of his upper arm above the cast twitched.

I lifted his head gently in my hands. His neck was so stiff it seemed that his head and torso were welded together.

I had just arrived at the hospital to relieve the regular surgeon. Dr. Huston wasted no time filling me in on this patient. "This is Kiran Kumar. He's about fourteen. He came a week ago with a broken arm and complications."

She asked the Nepali nurse to bring his X-rays and we scanned them together. I saw that both forearm bones were broken and there was another fracture just above the elbow.

She answered the rest of my questions quickly, before I had time to ask. The boy broke his arm in late morning and was carried to the hospital by fifteen men who ran for a whole day. They spelled each other off when the mountain pathways tired them. By the time they arrived in the evening, broken ends of Kiran Kumar's bones were sticking out through a dirty wound.

It must have been an incredibly difficult journey for the porters and the boy. Although the fracture had been treated properly, now something more serious than a broken bone was happening.

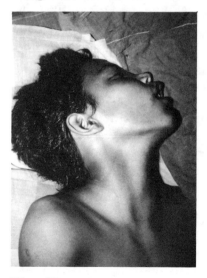

Kiran Kumar.

Helen proceeded with the briefing. "He's been running a fever all week and the pain at the fracture site seems to be getting worse. The first thing I noticed when I came in this morning was the twitching muscles and then the stiff neck."

We looked sombrely at each other. Helen quietly spoke the word we dreaded: "Tetanus."

Otherwise known as lockjaw, this disease was an almost certain death warrant. I had once seen, in Nepal, a newborn infant arched backwards in terrible spasms of tetanus. Healthy-looking at birth, the child died three days later—a preventable death, caused by using a contaminated *hansiya* (farm sickle) to cut the umbilical cord.

The boy's family read from our faces the seriousness of his condition, and gathered in silence around his cot. With strong, gentle fingers Helen tested his joints for muscle stiffness, at the same time speaking reassuringly in the Nepali language to the relatives. They answered her in tones that were just as subdued. I couldn't help but notice the respect they showed their doctor.

Helen, ready for another day, stands outside "the little thatched house."

"I can help with the care of the wound," I said, "but your experience with tetanus is far ahead of mine. What treatment do you have in mind?"

"We'll have to reduce any kind of stimulus—keep things dark and quiet. He'll need muscle-relaxant drugs, as well as analgesics for the pain."

I picked up his chart again, looking for clues to this life-threatening complication.

"I see he was started on penicillin as soon as he was admitted. What about anti-tetanus serum?"

Helen suddenly looked older and more weary. She sighed deeply and sank down on one of the benches.

"That's the saddest part," she said. "It was ordered by the doctor who admitted him, but because the family insisted that he had been inoculated as an infant, it was cancelled. So no anti-tetanus serum and no booster dose of toxoid. I've already written an order for the serum today."

Penicillin would destroy the tetanus bacteria that got in through the wound. We hoped the serum would knock out the powerful toxin that coursed through Kiran Kumar's bloodstream, but it was so little, so late.

Helen gave instructions in Nepali to the nurse to start an intravenous for the drugs.

"And *Bahini*," she said, using the Nepali term for younger sister, "please put down a stomach tube for feedings." If lockjaw came, his teeth would clench and he wouldn't be able to eat or drink.

The young boy was in good hands, and I headed for the operating room for the day's surgery. Most of my years in Nepal had been spent in the United Mission to Nepal's large hospital in the capital city of Kathmandu, but I always enjoyed coming to Amp Pipal. It was a marvel to me that this "heroic little hospital," as I took to calling it, could even exist, let alone provide the quality and quantity of medical work that took place under its corrugated aluminum roof.

It was already dark when my last case finished and I was able to check in on our brave young boy. The night watchman hadn't yet started the generator, so I pulled out a flashlight. Kiran Kumar looked stuporous but he wasn't having any seizures, a good sign that Helen's treatment was having an effect.

Because the hospital had only four trained nurses on staff, and only one at night, we counted, as usual, on the patient's family to help. Around the clock they watched Kiran Kumar, proving to be dependable and cooperative allies who immediately reported oncoming spasms to the nurse on duty. They never once threatened to take him home to the local *jankhri* (witch doctor).

Helen interwove medication and prayer, not once but many times, for her young patient. At first she asked Kiran Kumar's Hindu family if she could pray for him in the name of Jesus, and soon the parents asked her for these prayers.

Just as we were all beginning to feel encouraged by his progress, he suddenly got worse. I was at the far end of the hospital corridor when I heard a long, deep, mournful groan coming from the intensive care unit, and then silence. I raced toward the nursing station and joined Helen at Kiran's bedside. He was in the grip of a monstrous spasm, hardly able to breathe. His body was arched face up like a bridge, with only the back of his head and his heels touching the bed.

Helen was already injecting drugs, and with her lips tight she told me, "He's had two large doses of diazepam in twenty minutes. I just can't break the spasms. If they get any worse he'll stop breathing completely."

I asked what brought on the spasm. This one started, she said, as soon as the nurse pricked him to start a new intravenous. His sensitivity to stimuli was an enormous obstacle: he needed the IV but couldn't handle the prick of a needle, and he needed the stomach tube but it too was irritating and set off spasms. We also feared he'd develop pneumonia because the sedation depressed his breathing.

The following day, two new problems developed. It was his father, Indra Kumar, who first noticed the brownish stain on his son's plaster cast, unmistakable signs of infection draining from the cast's upper end. We trimmed away the cast to discover that the muscle spasms had driven the jagged broken bone of the upper fracture right through his skin. I removed the cast and cleaned up the wound, and we prayed even more earnestly. Barring a miracle, there wasn't a lot of cause for optimism.

For several days Kiran Kumar's life hung in the balance, and then, together, the staff and the family watched the tide begin to turn. Before I returned to Kathmandu, I heard Helen whisper softly by Kiran's bedside, "Thank you, Lord," and the day I left I was able to write on his chart, "He opened and closed his eyes in response to his mother's voice."

Our patient stayed under Helen's care for another month. In early spring, thirteen kilograms (thirty pounds) lighter, he was able to walk on his own the long trek home. A few months later he returned to visit the doctor who hadn't given up on him. His arm movements were certainly limited, but otherwise Kiran Kumar was a very bright and alert young boy with a healthy and hard-won respect for the gift of life.

On the day of my return to Kathmandu, I got up early, long before the sun's rays touched the aluminum roof of the hospital. Helen was up too, to say farewell and to give me a snack, a few stubby but delicious Nepali bananas and some peanuts, for the long hike to the road.

We waved goodbye and white-coated Helen strode off to begin another day's work in the primitive village tucked away in mountainous Nepal, her adopted home.

3

The Caring Tomboy

Helen Huston never has fit into a mould or conformed to anyone's prior expectations. Some call her free-spirited. Others have accepted that she is "an original." Born on September 20, 1927, in Innisfail, a town just off the Calgary-Edmonton highway, she grew healthy and strong in places like Wainwright and Rimbey, Alberta, small prairie towns where her father served as the United Church minister. Big sister Mary was three years older, then came James and Harold.

In her role as a "preacher's daughter," Helen Isabel Huston was entirely too bubbly and exuberant. Far from the shy and submissive girl one might have expected from the town of Rimbey in the depressed thirties, she was an unabashed tomboy. She seized every moment to play any kind of ball game, turning the walk to school with James into a chance to play catch, the last throw caught at the school door. When an ear infection kept her out of school, she decided this would not be lost time but an opportunity to learn to play the violin she had received for Christmas.

Will and Edith Huston were alternately puzzled and proud of their young daughter who never seemed to be intimidated by adults. She had a mind of her own and she spoke it freely.

Back in those days when families spent Sunday afternoons going for a drive together, the Hustons once passed a group of people huddled around a car on the shoulder of the road.

"Why don't you stop, Dad?" Helen pleaded. "Maybe they're in trouble and we can help them."

The Huston family in 1970. Back row: Harold, Helen, Mary, James. Front row: Will, Edith.

Her father, who had a heart as wide as the prairie horizon, explained that the people seemed to be managing fine on their own. He drove on past, and as dust and distance separated the two cars, he saw in his rear-view mirror his daughter's tear-filled eyes still looking back.

She knew about helping people, but some of life's lessons, especially in a school environment, were harder to learn. Her grade five report card noted that "Helen's writing is very careless," and "She whispers when she shouldn't." And the puzzling "If Helen did not work so hard, she would make better progress."

When she was interested, this pretty young girl with the bright blue eyes could learn anything, and it was certainly apparent that she had a natural interest in anatomy. When her youngest daughter was around, Edith Huston found cleaning a chicken to be far more than a routine job. With Helen watching over her shoulder, she was hard pressed to identify the organs, let alone describe the functions of the liver, gizzard and intestines.

The possibility of becoming a missionary doctor gradually took hold of Helen's imagination. Perhaps she was influenced by a young doctor who stayed with the Huston family for several months when she was seven years old, or the many missionaries from several continents who visited her home. Or maybe it was her first hospital stay, for acute appendicitis, at the age of ten, or hearing her father talk about the person he considered "the greatest man in the world today," the medical missionary to Africa, Dr. Albert Schweitzer.

But by the time she was twelve, she had made the dramatic announcement that she would be a medical missionary to China. It was a remote possibility for a girl from a poor prairie family in the thirties, and it was no surprise that, as she entered her teens, the dream faded.

Nothing specific had drawn her away from her goal. It was just that being a teenager kept her so busy, and there was a world war to finish, and wasn't it unrealistic to set her sights on being a doctor? She was sure she didn't have the "brains" to go to university. Besides, she didn't have Latin, and as if she needed another strike against her, she could hardly hope for the money to get through medical school.

Her lack of direction was compounded by a worse problem for a teenager. Although she was pretty and well liked, she was painfully aware that she wasn't "one of the gang." Her first boyfriend, a local farm boy named Roy, was a good friend and fun to be with, but somehow she seemed to be marching to a different drummer.

At school dances she felt awkward, out of step, and completely lacking in gracefulness and rhythm. When boys asked her to join them on the dance floor, she simply told them, "I'm sorry. I can't dance." She struggled with the realization that she was a misfit but was comforted by knowing that Jesus was a misfit too.

In the summer of 1945 seventeen-year-old Helen was determined to go to summer camp. There was no extra money in the Huston family account, so she put her best effort into writing a limerick for a radio contest and with the five-dollar first prize paid her own registration to the CGIT (Canadian Girls in Training) camp.

Newly graduated from high school and still puzzling about her future direction, she was in her room, packing her duffel bag to take to Sylvan Lake, when she heard the front door open. She looked downstairs to see her father disappearing into his study, and dropping everything, she bounded down the stairs to greet him.

Will Huston's life was an inspiration to his daughter. She knew he had grown up poor. During the Depression years, Will and Edith had struggled to make ends meet on a minister's salary, and that meant patches and hand-me-downs, and carrying water from a community pump across the street from the *Rimbey Record* newspaper building.

But even at their poorest, they were relatively well-off compared to her father's growing-up years. Will had been born before the turn of the century to a blind mother and a lame father. A special Sunday treat was a poached egg, which he shared with his brother. While still teenagers, the boys lost both parents. Will never forgot the kindness of the people of Forest, Ontario, who rallied around to help them get on their feet.

At the age of sixteen, he became a Christian and, after experiencing the savagery of the First World War, was more than ever ready to join the forces of reconciliation and peace. After a liberal theological education at the University of Toronto, he had married Edith Howard, and together they took their first pastoral charge, in faraway Athabasca, Alberta. For a long time after that, they moved every four years.

Poverty as a child had taught Will to be generous. When he was a pastor in Camrose, Alberta, in 1966, he happened to overhear a conversation in the bank. Members of his church had applied for a loan but were being turned down by the manager. As they turned to leave, he stepped forward and asked if he could help. "I have money sitting idle in this bank, and I'd like to put it to good use if you'll agree," he told the couple, lending them two thousand dollars interest-free.

As Helen breathlessly entered the study, Will looked with affection at his energetic daughter. He seemed to understand the confused state she was in and assured her that he and her mother would support her and encourage her in her life's plans. But only God could show her the direction, and perhaps, he said, He would show her while she was at camp. That's what he would pray for, he promised.

Sylvan Lake camp was a tightly packed, sun-filled schedule of games, swimming, hiking, and fireside singing and worship. But for Helen, who was by now only a few inches short of six feet, the greatest attraction was Elda Daniels, a tiny, sprightly missionary from Korea.

Helen became Elda's shadow. At mealtimes she would propel herself into position beside her to hear every word she spoke. She constantly probed for more answers when Elda wasn't speaking formally to the group. Helen was deeply impressed, partly by the obvious depth of Elda's faith, but mainly by her warmth and humility and her patience with Helen's bottomless pit of questions.

Long after darkness had fallen and the other campers had bedded down for the night, Helen walked along a stretch of lonely beach. Lost in her thoughts, she wasn't aware of a strong wind until thunder and lightning suddenly ripped the night with fury. Gale-force winds lashed the waves of the normally placid lake into foaming whitecaps.

Helen stood still on the stormy beach and, cupping her hands toward the sky, shouted at the top of her lungs, "Where are you, God? Speak to me. Show me your way for me!" In desperation, she called again and again, a tiny voice in the raging wilderness.

And then she was quiet, and the still, small voice of God seemed to answer her frantic cries. In a voice that seemed to come from deep inside her, she felt Him say, more clearly than if she had heard it with her ears, that yes, He wanted her to be a medical doctor.

Waves of exhilaration flooded her soul. This was the same plan that she had dreamed of years earlier, and she would do her best, she resolved, to follow it.

Any lingering doubts about the clear guidance, or any fears about following it, faded as soon as she stamped and sealed a letter to her parents. Her father had promised to pray, and he should be the first to know how his prayer was answered.

4

Training to be a Doctor

I heard Helen Huston for the first time before I actually saw her. Her laughter sounded so delightfully free and natural, and dispelled some of the gloom in the anatomy lab, a sombre sort of place at the best of times. Each morning, for two hours at a stretch, groups of four students gathered around cadavers to dissect muscles, nerves and blood vessels.

It was 1947 and Helen had been accepted into first year medicine at the University of Alberta as one of four women in a class of fifty-five students. This handsome young classmate, at five feet ten inches, as tall as many of the men, was found almost always in the centre of, and was usually the cause of, fun and excitement.

I was one of the serious war veterans in the freshman class. At least four years older than the kids fresh out of high school, we ex-servicemen outnumbered them six to one and were tough, no-nonsense competition for these younger students.

My education was provided by the Department of Veterans Affairs, but Helen's was covered by determination. With the small savings from her summer jobs, and with her mother's teaching salary going to pay her tuition and room and board, Helen had obtained the backing she needed to get through two years of pre-med at the University of Alberta, and now to finish her medical training.

She had expected her small-town education, with not a single Latin course, to be a roadblock, but after 1945 Latin was no longer a prerequisite. A new course was now offered to teach Latin medical terms in second-year pre-med.

People tended to notice Helen. Not only was her youthful beauty engaging, but her stature also attracted attention. Tall, large-boned and somewhat angular, she struck all of us as someone with a purpose. If there was something challenging to learn, she would learn it. If the superior thyroid artery had to be found, she would stay bent over her work until she found it. All her courses were pursued with the same enthusiasm and intensity. Yet there was an undeniable warmth and humanity about her.

Doubtless there were many fine features that made her attractive to men. One of her boyfriends was Harry, the chief cook at the Banff School of Fine Arts, where Helen held a summer job after second year. During the following year, she and Harry had great times together, biking and strolling along the banks of Edmonton's North Saskatchewan River. It was just a casual friendship, or so Helen thought until the day he asked her to marry him.

This was a dilemma. She really cared for him, but had he forgotten, she asked, that she was studying to be a missionary doctor in China?

"I haven't forgotten," he said. "I've thought a lot about it. Maybe I could be a missionary too, and go to China with you."

They walked on in silence. When they reached the steps of her boarding house, Helen turned to him. "You're a really fine man. It's hard for me to say no, but this does change things. I don't think we should keep seeing each other. However . . . can you just do me one small favour? It's going to be hard to break up, so can we keep on going out until after my exams?"

And Harry, being a great guy, laughed with her and answered, "Sure, Helen. We want you to pass those exams."

There were other men interested in Helen, including a man who sent a marriage proposal by mail, saying he liked the way she played the violin. The trouble with that proposal was rather obvious. Helen couldn't remember ever having met this fellow. She sent him a gently worded but emphatic refusal.

The romantic "marriage and family" side of life needed to be pushed to the side. Maybe someday there would be time and opportunity, but there were oceans to cross and mountains to climb first.

In the meantime, she was never short of friends. She developed a student-teacher rapport with our professor of zoology, Dr. William Rowan, a short, elderly man with eyes that looked out sharply at the lecture amphitheatre from behind thick glasses. He seemed to relish debunking religion of any kind, and particularly Christianity.

Helen saw another side of this professor and found him to be a man with a keen hunger for spiritual things. He would often invite her to have coffee with him in his office on the third floor of the medical building. There, surrounded by dusty books and jars of pickled frogs and dogfish, the zoology professor asked his young student questions about God.

The problem was, Helen didn't have the answers he was looking for. What she had was a lot of head knowledge about Christianity, but much of it was the "second-hand faith" of her parents, and she kept her heart at a safe distance. She knew her encounter with God at camp had been real, but why was it that she felt ill-at-ease with Christian fellow students and lacked the courage to stand up for her beliefs, and why was she often ashamed to admit she was a minister's daughter?

For both Dr. Rowan and Helen, this was a time for searching and not finding. Deep in Helen's heart, there was a yearning and a hunger for God. But it was as if a heavy black curtain kept light from reaching her.

Her camaraderie with Dr. Rowan represented the serious side of Helen. Others saw the lighter side. A classmate who was afraid to hitchhike to classes at the university was as confident as could be when she thumbed with Helen. Helen was the teammate you wanted on your side during a snowball fight, and she could render strange and original versions of arias from *La Traviata* from the shower.

I think I missed much by not getting to know Helen Huston well during our four years in many of the same classes. But of course she was so young, and I was so wise and experienced! Farther down the road our paths would connect again, and things would be different.

*****

The groundwork was complete. Helen was a graduate of the University of Alberta Faculty of Medicine, class of '51. On a sunny day in May she donned cap and gown with her fifty-four classmates at a solemn convocation ceremony and received the right hand of congratulation from the university chancellor, Dr. G. Fred McNally.

Helen Huston, graduate in Medicine, May, 1951.

On July 1, she joined that group of pale-faced, haggard interns who found themselves immersed up to their eyebrows in medical problems. She was looking for first-hand experience in the management of illnesses and injuries, but hadn't bargained for being on the bottom rung of the medical ladder. As a lowly junior intern she spent a year at the Royal Alexandra Hospital in Edmonton, rotating through several of the clinical departments. But she didn't get much surgical experience—a cause for concern because one can't be a missionary doctor without surgery.

And it wasn't long before she noticed a gaping hole in her training. How was she to meet the desperate plight of the seriously ill and dying? How was she to act? What was she to say to them? Would little things, like gentle words and the touch of a comforting hand, be enough?

Did praying for sick people fit in anywhere? The curriculum designers and clinical teachers had scoffed at prayer. Medicine was a science, they said.

All these questions weighed heavily upon her the night they brought a young man into emergency after a car accident. Severely brain injured, he was unconscious and bleeding from one ear. When he stopped breathing, another doctor introduced a tube into his windpipe

17

so air could be forced into his lungs. The relatives were informed that there was virtually no hope, and the doctor went home for the night, leaving the patient in Helen's trained but inexperienced hands.

She stayed beside the comatose patient all night, squeezing the bag every few seconds to inflate his lungs. The whole night she prayed fervently that God would save this young life. Surely a head injury was not too difficult for the Creator of the universe to heal. If she did her part by staying with him all night, would God not do the miraculous and save his life?

Helen was still at her post when the neurosurgeon returned in the morning. She was persuaded to give up and remove the bag and tube. Within a few minutes the young man's heart stopped beating and she pulled a white sheet over his face, questions as heavy as lead weights filling her tired mind. She had done her level best. Where had God been? The question remained unanswered.

Permanent job offers began to come in months before the year's internship ended. She accepted a short-term locum, replacing a doctor taking a holiday from her practice. She lived in the doctor's home, which became the gathering place for a host of new friends, and rode to house calls on her bike.

The locum completed, she was off to Vancouver General Hospital on July 1, 1952, as assistant resident in surgery, an opportunity to get solid practical exposure to the basics of surgery in Canada.

She was still determined to be a medical missionary, but her focus shifted from China, where borders were closed after the Communist revolution of 1949. The Hustons had United Church missionary friends in India, and that is where she now set her sights. Her application for overseas service was sent to the Mission Board of the United Church of Canada.

One of her new friends in Vancouver was Cathie Nicoll, a staff worker with Inter-Varsity Christian Fellowship. Cathie saw hundreds of young people in the course of a year, but Helen impressed her immediately as the "strong young woman with the very alive face."

They sat down together for tea one Sunday afternoon, after a crowd of students had left. Cathie watched Helen's face as she listened to her plans to go to India as a medical missionary. Then, point-blank, she asked a question. "Apart from your medical knowledge, Helen, what do you plan to take with you?"

There was a silence before Helen spoke. "I know what you're getting at. I admit I'm not sure about Christianity or even about my own spiritual life right now. But I think maybe it's enough that I can help the people of India as a doctor."

That idealism and humanitarian attitude were admirable strengths to take to India, Cathie conceded, but she asked, "Is that enough?"

Helen couldn't shake the question. It hung over her the spring day of 1953 when she appeared before an examining board in Toronto, as a candidate for missionary service. For these friendly, courteous people, she appeared to have all the right answers. Some interviewers almost got her laughing, like the psychiatrist who asked the un-anticipated "Do you think you can cope with insects and heat and bad smells?"

A thorough physical examination followed, at which she felt she had to divulge that she had developed a heart condition called paroxysmal auricular tachycardia (fluttering heartbeat) in her early teens. The cardiologist who was consulted concluded that her fluttering heart was something she could live with.

She had passed through all the gates. She was commissioned in July, 1953 as a United Church medical missionary in the little church in south Calgary where her father served as minister.

Helen spoke during the service and said all the things that were expected of a well-trained Christian about to set out for the mission field. The words were well practised and came freely and naturally.

But deep within her was a gnawing uneasiness. She had many good things to take with her to India. But were they enough?

5

Venturing into the Far East

The SS Empress of France cast off her moorings from Montreal harbour on a steamy September day in 1953. Looking confident and dignified, Helen kept her poise in the centre of a circle of friends and family at dockside.

But on board, as the tiny figures on the wharf disappeared from view, she felt incredibly lonely and isolated. She watched her family and country being slowly swallowed up by the soft mist, and, lost in the widening distance, she simply could not stop the flow of hot tears running down her cheeks.

She was still leaning against the ship's railing when an arm went around her waist. Mildred Cates, a United Church missionary heading to India for her fifth term, and another friend, Muriel Bamford, became Helen's companions and encouragers for the first leg of the long trip, across the choppy North Atlantic for three weeks in England.

She then boarded the SS Batory, a Polish vessel bound for Bombay. It would take three weeks, via the Strait of Gibraltar and the Suez Canal, but those three weeks would include a side trip to Cairo.

She wrote to her friends back home: *"What an amazing experience to sit on a camel, look out on the great Sahara, view the pyramids and the Sphinx and ponder these relics of truly ancient history. Such a contrast between this five thousand-year-old culture and Rimbey and other Alberta towns where I grew up."*

At Montreal on the SS Empress of France, September 4, 1953.
Left to right: Muriel Bamford, Helen Huston, Mildred Cates.

The greatest thrill in her brief exposure to Egypt's past awaited her in the Museum of Antiquities in Cairo. She looked intently into the glass case which held the mummy of Rameses the Great, the "Pharaoh of the Oppression" who, to his peril, had resisted Moses' plea to "Let my people go." All that was left of this once-powerful man, so desperately seeking immortality for himself, were his shrivelled and desiccated mummified remains.

She rejoined the SS Batory, that seemed to be a mini United Nations with Indians making up half the complement of passengers. An unexpected bonus was a treasure of human cargo that included more than two hundred missionaries heading for points overseas. The many who had years of experience in Asian countries had encouragement and sound advice for her. Others who were taking that same first step into the unknown helped her just as much by matching their qualms and fears with hers.

Daily periods for Bible study and worship filled one of the ship's recreation rooms to capacity, and Helen was normally glad to participate. But one session in particular made her feel totally uncomfortable. Seated, almost hiding, at the back of the room, she listened to a young woman from Coventry, England, who quietly shared with them the message of Jesus as the good Shepherd who gave His life for the sheep. It sent Helen's mind into turmoil. She was afraid that she might scream out loud and shatter the stillness of the meeting.

"If only I could believe as that girl does," she agonized inwardly. "I want to, but I can't. I can't. I can't!"

*****

Soon after dawn on October 18 the ocean liner steamed into Bombay harbour, the "Gateway to India." No amount of advance warning could have prepared Helen for the bombardment of sights, sounds and smells which faced her in the Indian metropolis.

Bicycles and bullock carts, bells and horns, rickshaws and rickety buses, coolies walking with great loads perched on their heads, graceful ladies dressed in saris, holy men with beards, scantily clad children—it was sensory overload for a young woman from the quiet prairies.

She headed immediately out of Bombay for Allahabad where she joined thirty-five doctors, nurses, teachers and preachers, all new to India, and began immediately to learn the difficult Hindi language. Classroom lessons in the morning introduced her to new sounds and sentence structures, and in the afternoons she and a *pandit* (teacher) practised proper pronunciation of Hindi expressions.

Life at the Allahabad Language School was planned to include fun and recreation: social events of all kinds, and activities such as basketball, volleyball and table tennis. She appreciated her living quarters, which weren't lavish but were certainly comfortable.

Ironically, the comfort made her feel uncomfortable. Down the road from the school, people lived in shacks with mud floors. And as she ate her third square meal of the day, she couldn't get her mind off the adults and children she had seen only hours before, foraging for food in garbage dumps.

She joined several other language students who deliberately refused frills and luxuries and took on menial tasks in a symbolic attempt to narrow the gap that separated them from the destitute people who lived on the streets outside their door. Language school administrators respected the idealism of the students, but the break with tradition was considered a rebellion. Helen and her friends stood their ground, saying they would feel like hypocrites if they called themselves Christians and clung to luxuries in the midst of a sea of poverty.

For Helen, the self-imposed devotion to simplicity was there to stay. A dented and battered tin trunk that long ago could, and probably should have been replaced by something a little more solid, has survived from that time, marking the start of the simple life that Helen chose for herself back in Allahabad.

Allahabad, 1953–54. Some of the class and pandits (language teachers). Helen, third from right. Jay Story, third from left.

For part of the term, Helen's classmates were Dr. Carl Friedericks and his wife, Betty. They left language study for three weeks to make a trip into a remote little country called Nepal and came back to Allahabad bubbling over with superlatives about the land and the people. Helen stood nearby while they described the highest, most awesome mountains they had ever seen, beyond their wildest imaginations, and the health problems of the country that were as massive as the mountains.

"I saw typhoid and worms and goitres like I've never seen before. There's no health care there, and that's why we're going back as soon as we can," said Carl and, turning to Helen, added, "I could sure use another good doctor there."

Helen smiled. "Sorry, Carl," she said, "but I've already committed myself to doing what I can here in India. It does sound interesting though." And the subject of Nepal was dismissed—for a time.

Understanding Indian culture and religion was challenge enough for Helen.

Her Indian pandits were, almost without exception, educated and intelligent men, and she found them to be tolerant and remarkably friendly. But some aspects of the Hindu religion were difficult to understand and, when they seemed cruel, difficult to accept.

Street beggars were not considered a nuisance by most Indians; giving alms to a beggar had some advantages—the action gained merit for the next life.

One pandit whom she had considered so tolerant shocked her at class one day by calling his daughter a curse. She often let differences pass, but this remark Helen couldn't ignore. "I'm the daughter of my father," she said. "Am I a curse to him?"

He hastened to explain that she was not a curse to her father because she was not costing him money.

"Next week I'm going home to arrange for my daughter's wedding," he said. "I'll have to pay the groom's father a thousand rupees. I'll be responsible for all the expenses of the wedding and will be expected to buy furnishings for their household. It will cost four months' salary before my share is paid."

Perhaps fathers did resent being trapped by Hindu marriage traditions, Helen thought, but then it was the traditions, not the daughters, that were the curse.

During language study, she had her first introduction to the Indian caste system that categorized a person's worth according to a rigid hierarchy.

India by this time had many well-trained medical doctors, but her teacher told her how *vaidya* healers, practitioners of folk medicine, could make a diagnosis simply by feeling the pulse in the patient's wrist.

"I know of a high-caste *vaidya*," he told her, "who had a low-caste woman come to his clinic for help. He couldn't touch her and he didn't want to look at her, so he had her stay outside his office door. He sent out the end of a thread and told her to wrap the thread around her wrist several times. Then he told her to send the other end back to him. He held the thread, made the right diagnosis and cured her."

Helen took a deep breath and kept silent. But inwardly she quivered a bit and wondered what opinion her professor of internal medicine would have had on the *vaidya's* approach.

Tragedy struck one of the pandits during Helen's stay at language school. His wife, a lovely woman with two small children, was cooking rice for her family one evening when her sari touched the open fire, and in an instant she was engulfed in flames. She was rushed to hospital, but the third degree burns were too extensive, and she died three days later.

The sorrow of her death became Helen's first experience with Hindu funeral rites. She described them clearly.

The woman was lying, draped in a purple cloth, on the sand near the river, carried there by the language teachers. There was no show of emotion as her husband gathered straw in a pile, then kindling, then large pieces of wood to a height of about three feet. He then laid the body gently on the funeral pyre, applied some sacred ointment with his hands, and then sprinkled sandalwood powder. He placed on the pyre three loaves of dough, for her to eat in the next life.

Then while a holy man chanted, he walked around the pyre several times, carrying a burning torch, and pointing it towards her body. Finally the husband touched her face lightly with his hand and set fire to the pyre.

At the end, the ashes were committed to the holy waters of the Ganges, assuring her a safe passage to the next life.

6

Tragedy at the Kumbh Mela

Helen's stay in Allahabad coincided with Maha Kumbh Mela, a Hindu holy festival that a *National Geographic* reporter judged as perhaps "the largest periodic assemblage of human beings on the planet."

Held about every twelve years—the time is calculated by astrologers—millions of Hindus of all castes, classes, doctrines and sects come together near the city of Allahabad for a mass immersion ritual. This year the position of the stars pointed to the most auspicious and holy Kumbh Mela festival in 108 years.

Hindus believe that four drops of the nectar of immortality fell to earth, making four sacred places. The holiest of the four is the site of the Kumbh Mela. At this sacred time and place, they believe worshippers can wash away the sins of all their past lives and pray to escape the cycle of endless reincarnation.

Allahabad would soon be in the centre of a massive explosion of pilgrims, and authorities of the city trembled as they anticipated the climax of the festival. On February 3 they expected five million Hindus to converge in one area—the confluence of the Jamna, the Ganges and the secret underground Saraswati rivers.

Before the festival, health authorities asked at the language school for medical personnel to work at first-aid posts close to the rivers. Helen volunteered, and at 5 a.m. on February 3 she joined the swarm of people heading toward the river junction. A pandit and two co-workers accompanied her, but they were soon locked into the traffic jam and had to abandon their rickshaw to join the unbroken movement of people.

Kumbh Mela. Some of the five million pilgrims who flocked to the river.

Women carried babies on their hips. Old men hung on to sons and moved forward bravely for this climax of their spiritual odyssey. Bearing loads on their heads, younger men and women revelled in the adventure. Helen was hemmed in by a sea of people, as far as her eye could see. To the horizon and beyond, it seemed no one could move in any direction. The tide of solid humanity occupied every single square inch of ground as the throngs of people shouted again and again, *"Ganga Ma-Ki Jai!"* (Victory to Mother Ganges).

Pushed forward with the surge of pilgrims, she was close to her assigned first-aid post. Using her few Hindi words and doggedly inching onward, she managed to reach the entrance of the makeshift tent, marvelling that this flimsy structure hadn't been trampled underfoot.

For two hours she worked as the post doctor, attending to various minor problems, when suddenly a policeman burst into the tent.

"Come quickly," he shouted. "There's an emergency—a terrible accident!"

Grabbing a medical bag, she followed him out of the tent with several stretcher bearers in tow. They all stuck as close as they could to the baton-swinging policeman, who forged a path through the mob.

As they crested a hill, the doctor and medical workers stopped cold. Helen's eyes were riveted on the tragic scene that stretched out in front of her. A huge section of the crowd—hundreds of people—was lying on the ground, some writhing in agony, others motionless. These people had been crushed at the base of a slippery incline.

The air was filled with sounds Helen had never even imagined and would never forget—the wailing and screaming of hundreds of injured, helpless and bewildered people. Above the noise, the policeman shouted. He explained that a procession of *Sadhus* (holy men) on elephants had come trotting up from one side of the brow of the hill and then passed by. To fill in the gap left in the elephants' wake, the colossal crowd had swept forward like an angry tidal wave. People in front slid down the side of the hill, slippery from heavy rains. Thousands lost their balance and fell headlong, crushing the crowd below.

Policemen and army reinforcements already at the scene struggled to restore a semblance of order, but the sheer numbers of people were too much. They tried to form a human barricade to keep the uninjured out of the way, but there was no controlling the masses of hysterical, wailing people pushing through and pleading for help for their family and friends.

Helen was the only doctor on the scene. She shook off her fear and moved into action quickly, assessing the state of the injured and selecting the most seriously hurt to be carried away by stretcher.

Then she began a count of the dead. More than four hundred times she had to call out the harsh Hindi word, *mar'e*, for sobbing relatives who begged her to do something, anything. She wanted to say "I'm afraid there's no heartbeat," or "I'm so sorry, but your child cannot be saved," but "dead" was all she knew.

Lying helter-skelter in the mud, the bodies were being trampled and mutilated by the writhing crowd. She asked for help from the able-bodied people around the scene, but one man after another refused. If they touched a dead body on such a holy occasion, they would bring a curse upon themselves.

After exhausting hours on the hillside, moving the bodies herself and having the injured carried to the first-aid post, Helen made her way slowly against the human current, back to the post. There she began to attend to the most serious injuries, putting out of her mind the pile of bodies that she had left in the open.

She hadn't been back at the tent more than a few minutes when the flap was thrown open and in walked the pandit who had been her companion earlier in the morning. She leapt up. Here was hope. This man was her trusted friend and a rational thinker. Surely he would help her, at least by translating at the scene of the disaster.

"I'm sorry. I can't," he told her calmly. "But don't worry about these people who died, because they are fortunate. Anyone who dies on a pilgrimage goes straight to heaven."

7

The Road to Damascus

The students at language school were divided into two camps, so to speak. One camp stood on solid ground spiritually and had good news to tell others. The other camp had no such good news. Helen saw them as the "haves" and the "have-nots."

She knew she belonged to the have-nots. She felt comfortable with the first group but wasn't sure she ever could or ever would belong to it. On this subject, her mind was a tangled web. She desperately wanted to believe one moment. Then she felt sorry for herself because she couldn't believe.

The Bible was a major hang-up. In medical school Dr. Rowan had pointed out how the Genesis story of creation was simply unacceptable, given the known age of the earth revealed by scientific methods. How much could one honestly be expected to believe such stories as Eve being formed from Adam's rib?

Questioning parts of the Bible was just reflecting her upbringing. "We just don't believe that way in our church," she told others, and besides, she argued in her mind: it just doesn't make sense. God has given me a brain and he means for me to use it.

Helen dashed into the dining room one evening, late as usual, for supper, and sat down opposite Jay Story, a young United Church minister at the language school. As they ate their curried rice meal, they talked casually about Hindi and pandits and mail from home. Then, after a pause, Jay abruptly changed the subject.

"I've been watching you over these weeks, Helen," he said. "Somehow I get the feeling you're wrestling with the same kinds of doubts and uncertainties that I struggled with a few years ago. Do you mind if I ask you . . . where do you stand in your spiritual journey? I mean, how much does the Lord mean to you?"

Helen slowly put down her cup of *chai* (tea) but could not raise her eyes to answer his question. Still, she felt the time had come to admit her feelings.

"I must confess that you're right," she said. "I am wrestling. I believe in God and I'm ready to serve Him here in India. But to tell the truth, I feel kind of empty and hollow inside."

She told Jay that she believed Jesus was the Son of God, but added, "I can't understand the cross. It's a mystery to me. It bothers me to tell you that I'm in such a pitiful state, but it's true."

Jay understood. "I've been on the same road," he said, "and I know how you feel. I have a little booklet that helped me. It was written thirty years ago, but I think you may find it helpful." He handed her a copy of *The Reason Why*, got up and left.

At her first opportunity the next day, Helen scanned the little booklet. Its message seemed quite innocuous and straightforward until she reached the part about the "first and greatest commandment."

She picked up her Bible and found Jesus' answer in chapter 22 of Matthew's gospel. "You shall love the Lord your God with all your heart and with all your soul and with all your mind."

Then the booklet asked a simple question that pierced her heart: "Have you ever broken this commandment?"

A stormy, turbulent week followed. The question tormented her, and if it hadn't been for a retreat for language students the following weekend, she might have reached the breaking point.

On the spacious grounds of the retreat centre, she found a secluded place under a great flowering tree and there stopped running from that simple question. To be true to her own heart, she knew how she would have to answer. She had not only broken the first and greatest commandment in her lifetime, but she had never kept it. Helen Isabel Huston had been the supreme and unrivalled centre of her life.

On that Palm Sunday of 1954, Helen came face to face with the worst and the best of revelations. The worst, that she was as guilty of sin and selfishness as anyone else in the world. No wonder God seemed so far away.

And then the best. She could be freed from the guilt of sin and be restored to a right relationship with God only by accepting Jesus as her Saviour. In her mind's eye she saw Him on the cross and realized His suffering was for her. She wept, fell on her knees and cried out, "What shall I do?"

Suddenly she understood. She asked God to forgive her. Nothing more. As she stayed still and quiet under the flowering tree, she suddenly became aware of a strange peace. It seemed that a weight had fallen from her shoulders. She was overwhelmed by the wondrous love of God for her—love that would sustain her and strengthen her in the tempestuous years to follow.

In her next letter to her parents, Helen wrote, "I feel that this term has meant more to me in spiritual growth than in any other way. I now feel sure that we must continually be of a broken and contrite heart. If God is really like Jesus, He can have my heart!"

From Palm Sunday, 1954, Helen was different.

Jay Story, who knew the old and the new Helen, noticed the change: "Helen's whole life received a new impetus and sense of direction, as well as a whole new set of values and standards. She was no longer merely a doctor ministering to physical needs of the poor and destitute, but an ambassador of Christ with a deep concern for the spiritual and eternal welfare of those whom she served."

Thirty years after that transformation, he wrote, "I do not find any evidence of her reneging on the commitment she made to Jesus. If anything, Helen is deeper and more mature than ever, and still able to listen and learn."

She was still Helen, but now she was free!

With a new spring in her stride, Helen left hot and humid Allahabad for higher ground.

Landour in the hills northeast of Delhi reminded her of the foothills of the Canadian Rockies. At an altitude of 7,200 feet breezes of fresh, cool air blew across hills and ridges covered with fir and pine trees. From her window she looked down upon the city of Dehra Dun and the steamy plains, and, toward the northeast, up to the great white, craggy Himalayan Mountains.

Language School, Landour, India, 1954. Fellow student Nora Vickers (on left) put forward Helen's name, resulting in a telegram calling her to Nepal in 1955.

She dived into language study intensely, determined to master Hindi so she would never again be as powerless as she had been at the Kumbh Mela tragedy.

On October 1, 1954 with formal language study completed, Helen left Landour for the Indore hospital and training centre down on the plains. Here she was to get practical in-hospital experience in tropical medicine. It would mean learning by seeing, reading and doing—and it would certainly take time.

She was given all of six weeks before being called on to take charge of the 35-bed hospital at Dhar some forty miles away. Apart from one lab technician, not another person in the hospital could speak English, and Helen's working knowledge of Hindi was still shaky. She would be the only doctor for the entire hospital. On final rounds with the Indian doctor she was replacing, anxiety rose even higher. The medicines here were new and strange, and diseases like typhoid and malaria hadn't been part of her training.

But the ultimate panic set in as soon as the Indian lady doctor informed her that one surgical operation she would have to perform often would be a craniotomy. Helen was shaken to the core. A craniotomy was a delicate open-skull operation which Helen had never even seen performed, much less attempted herself.

The minute she was able to excuse herself, she made her way home where she could be alone, closed the door, leaned against the wall and burst into tears. How could she possibly cope alone with such immense responsibility? Who could help her? It was a long time before she reached for her Bible, but when she finally did, in desperation, she drank in these words of the prophet Isaiah: *"He gives strength to the weary and increases the power of the weak. . . . They who hope in the Lord will renew their strength. They will soar on wings like eagles; they will run and not grow weary, they will walk and not be faint."*

That desperate day transformed Helen. She had no doubt that God had spoken. The next morning she could cheerfully say goodbye to Dr. Matthew.

And so began a stressful six-week period with Helen feeling confident that she would be given strength over and above her own resources. It was also an enormous relief to discover, that same morning, that the operation referred to by the doctor was really not a craniotomy. The doctor had meant to use a similar-sounding medical term for an operation to remove the dead baby from a woman who had come to hospital late in obstructed labour. This was more familiar territory and something she could handle.

For the month and a half, she bore a heavy load. But there were peaks of joy. After only a few days of decent food and medical treatment, several sickly and malnourished infants gained weight and strength. One six-month-old malnourished baby named Manohar weighed less than five pounds when he was brought to Dr. Helen. Pale, weak and feverish, at first he had refused food, but after the first few forced feedings he became ravenously hungry and his emaciated body began to fill out. Manohar survived.

But not all babies did. Sundar, a nineteen-year-old pregnant woman almost at term, came to the hospital on a Thursday. Weak and dehydrated with dysentery, she went into labour on Saturday and delivered a son. But her child was sickly and listless and died when only a few days old. Just as Sundar was beginning to regain strength after the birth, her husband came for her.

He stopped Dr. Helen in the hospital corridor. "I'm taking her home," he told her. "She doesn't need to stay here any longer."

Helen pleaded with him. "Don't take her just yet, please! She is still very weak after the delivery, and she still needs more treatment for the dysentery. Give her at least a few more days."

But the husband had made up his mind. "I've already spent enough money on her. Besides, if she can't give me a son that lives, I'll take another wife."

Helen watched as an uncomplaining Sundar gathered up her belongings and walked off behind her husband. No wonder that many village women feared more than anything else the inability to bear children, especially sons.

After Dhar, something changed inside Helen. She felt like a misfit again. She no longer felt as comfortable working at the large medical institution at Indore, with so many Indian and missionary doctors, where there were vague lines between each one's duties and responsibilities. She said, "I just couldn't seem to get my teeth into the job."

Then a letter came—a letter that would dramatically change her life. It came from Nepal on January 3, 1955. From the new United Mission to Nepal, the request was straightforward: *"We urgently need a doctor to replace Dr. Bethel Fleming in the old cholera hospital in Kathmandu. Can you possibly come for three months?"*

On the same morning, Helen had prayed, "Lord, please show me how to fit in here at Indore, or send me somewhere else!"

8

The Mysterious Himalayan Kingdom

Helen had just been invited to work in one of the most intriguing places on the face of the earth. A country long forbidden to foreigners, Nepal is aptly called "the last home of mystery."

This country, where one can step in and out of centuries many times in a day, offers unparalleled adventure. Its lands are tightly squeezed between walls of ranges and peaks that resemble the waves of an ocean. The country is a collision point, crushed between the two giants of India and China.

Along its northern border with Tibet, Nepal's 800-kilometre border is fortified by the Himalayan Mountains, the highest range in the world, and eight of the ten highest mountains in the world. The most famous is Mount Everest, at more than 8,800 metres.

Along its southern border with India, the terrain is as flat as the plains. Within a narrow span of about 200 kilometres from north to south, the climate changes from frigid and subarctic to steamy and tropical. Every conceivable kind of climatic condition lies between these extremes. It has been said that the only geographic and climatic area even remotely comparable to the diversity found in Nepal is British Columbia, Canada.

Helen's destination was Kathmandu, Nepal's capital city, which lay in the middle range, in a wide, oval valley shaped like a large bowl. Long ago, legends say, a lake covered this valley floor.

Major trade routes linking the empires of India with those of Tibet and China intersected in this city and created a once-powerful trade centre.

Nepal is set apart from other countries of the world by the mountains which create a natural fortress. But it is also set apart by the fortress mentality and isolationist course its leaders chose. Nepal remained closed to foreigners and foreign influence for more than one hundred years.

While the rest of the world moved on, many countries making progress even through colonial influence, the tiny kingdoms that now make up Nepal slept through a Rip Van Winkle time warp. The land stood still and froze into a feudal system in which poverty and disease thrived. Apart from royalty and a privileged elite, the people lived a dim existence, trapped in the Middle Ages.

When Helen first visited Nepal, about 8.5 million people lived within the borders of the land-locked country. More than ninety percent of the population made their living from subsistence farming, and for most of them, life was an unending series of struggles.

Only a few years earlier, in 1951, a bloodless revolution had restored the monarchy from the rule of the powerful and despotic Rana family to repatriated King Tribhuvan. The king removed some of the barriers which had locked the country in isolation for a century. But the long-standing fear and suspicion of foreigners were not instantly erased. The country resisted throwing open the doors to outsiders who might threaten the state religion of Hinduism. Christian missionaries were highly suspect.

But foreign aid and assistance were desperately needed, and Christian missions bringing schools, hospitals and agricultural and technical training could not be refused. From the time the borders were opened until today, foreign aid has been Nepal's chief source of income. Tourism is second, and growing.

One of the earliest Christian missionaries, Carl Friedericks, described Nepal as a "country of hills and problems." The hills, though magnificent, were "not easy to live with" and posed major challenges for transportation and communication systems. Other problems in the fourth poorest country in the world were formidable: malnutrition and starvation, poverty, illiteracy, superstition, rampant disease, early death. . . . There seemed to be no end.

Travel out of the valley and into the mountains was a supreme test of strength and endurance. Mountain-climbing expeditions had to conquer rugged terrain, weather, massive logistic problems of communication, supply, movement and health, and the mountains themselves.

From her first glimpse of the great white Himalayas from the Landour, India, side, Helen had felt drawn to these hills. She would need more than human inner strength to work in a country so bowed down with staggering problems. But the immense problems were precisely what attracted her. She wanted to be where she was most needed.

*****

On a cloudless January morning, Helen flew from Patna, India into Kathmandu, along the indescribable Himalayas—a sea of craggy, snow-covered peaks that soared unbelievably into the sky.

It all seemed like a dream, but later, a rough landing on the grassy runway quickly jolted her back to reality.

There was another jolt in store—the airport terminal consisted of three bamboo walls plastered with mud, the fourth side was open and no floor.

First impressions of this city of the bizarre and strange immediately brought to Helen's mind the words of the poet Rudyard Kipling, who wrote, "And the wildest dreams of Kew are the facts of Kathmandu."

Becky Grimsrud, an American nurse and Eunice Stevens, a British lab technician, were at the airport to meet her. They piled her bags into the back of a red jeep and bounced over rough and rutted roads until they reached the main urban area and the few roads that were paved.

How different it seemed from India. It was quite cool, even chilly. The city was surrounded by a rim of high hills. They bounced into the city where she saw a bizarre collection of two- and three-storey brick buildings intermingled with makeshift shacks and hovels. The occasional ornate palaces surrounded by formal gardens and high fences were the homes of the aristocracy.

As in India, cows wandered freely over the roads, and vehicles had to dodge animals, people, bicycles. Helen asked Becky why there were hardly any cars on the streets.

It was astonishing, Becky said, that there were any cars at all. Every vehicle had to be carried into Kathmandu. Strong beams secured to each car had been lifted and supported by forty men who walked overland from the end of the road twenty miles outside the city. There were only twenty-six vehicles in the city.

Helen was struck by the vast number of Hindu temples, shrines and idols lining the streets, each one splattered with red dye and flower petals by people doing *puja* (worship). Buddhist temples were also part of the landscape.

Early morning street scene in Patan Durbar Square, Kathmandu.

She had come to Nepal to replace Dr. Bethel Fleming of the United Mission for three months. Her duties would involve the medical and administrative work of the "cholera hospital" and attendance at clinics outside the city. The nurses were especially glad to welcome the young Canadian doctor, they had carried on without a doctor for several weeks.

On the misty morning of January 30, 1955, Helen set out on foot for the old cholera hospital at Teku for her first day on the job. She followed a path which ran between fields of winter wheat and then along an uneven track leading up to a rickety and antiquated suspension bridge. Striding briskly across the bridge, she glanced down at the waters of the Bagmati River.

She wondered how bathing in this murky, sluggish stream could be considered by Hindus a purification rite. On the shore, smoke rose from a cremation on one of the burning ghats. She paused for an instant, offered a prayer for the departed soul, and finished her trip to the hospital.

The Mission used one-half of the hospital. The Ministry of Health kept the other half, in case another cholera epidemic would occur. Epidemics seemed to strike every three to four years. The entire hospital would be needed if another one struck.

The old building hardly deserved to be called a hospital. It consisted of a ward with fifteen beds, a central waiting room, an examining room, a delivery room, a tiny lab and a small operating room. The fifteen beds were usually filled, and the small waiting room crowded with people waiting to be seen.

This particular hospital had been designated to serve women and children, but one evening a young man from South India arrived for emergency help. George John had all the signs and symptoms of acute appendicitis. He had refused to go to the government hospital in downtown Kathmandu. He was well aware of the risks of any operation in this primitive setting with only the most basic of operating instruments, but he had heard of Dr. Helen and had trust in her.

Helen herself still did not feel confident doing surgery, but if the condition was life-threatening she would get on with the job. With a couple of flashlights to illuminate the operating field, she performed the surgery to remove George John's inflamed appendix. Her patient recovered well—a surgical success—but he had to spend his post-operative days out on the porch, away from the women and children.

Other days brought crushing tragedies. Near the end of one long day's work, Helen leaned down to take the pulse of a young woman who had been carried to the hospital. Clammy and in shock, she had been in labour for five days and nights. Helen tried to resuscitate her with fluids and then gently delivered the dead baby. But when she reached up to draw down the placenta, she discovered the frightful truth that the woman's uterus had ruptured. She could do nothing to save the mother's life.

When her patient's weak pulse finally disappeared during the night, Helen wept. Her old professor of obstetrics had been right. He had warned his students that the death of a mother in labour is one of the most cruel blows a doctor has to endure.

Three times a week, Helen travelled with a nurse to small clinics outside the city in the Kathmandu Valley. The existing clinics set up by Dr. Bethel Fleming seemed to grow weekly, and she added another at a village about six miles from the city, to try to keep pace with the staggering need for health care that far exceeded what she had seen in India.

In the hillside town of Kirtipur, she saw scores of adults whose faces bore the ugly scars of smallpox, and she learned that a smallpox epidemic had struck the community several years earlier. People still lived in dread of the disease. Just a stone's throw from the two-thousand-year-old Buddhist shrine, Swayambhunath, stood a small ornate temple erected to the goddess of smallpox. Helen saw people lining up to pay homage to this deity with offerings of rice, spices and flowers.

She hadn't expected to find any Christian believers in Nepal and was pleasantly surprised to meet Gyani, a young assistant nurse at the cholera hospital who hadn't been deterred even though she had suffered for becoming a Christian.

Helen was also delighted to meet Colonel Sahib, a former army officer who had been converted at the border town of Raxaul before returning home to Kathmandu a changed man. He quickly learned how dangerous it was to speak openly about his new-found faith but took the risk of opening his home for prayer and Bible study. The young Canadian doctor was one who came often to his door.

She also met a number of committed South Indian Christians in Kathmandu, including C.K. Attialy and his family. C.K.'s story was an amazing one. Years before in South India, his mother had heard an address by the celebrated Indian preacher-evangelist Sadhu Sundar Singh. As she listened to the good news he relayed, she offered her unborn child to God to tell the same good news in the closed land of Nepal. When C.K. became a teenager, she told him about her promise. After his mother's death, he travelled to northeastern India to learn the Nepali language and then took for his own the vow she had made. A few weeks after meeting C.K. and his wife, Helen delivered their first-born son at the cholera hospital.

On a historic day in March, Helen finished her clinic work by mid-afternoon and, still wearing her hospital garb, raced off to join a huge milling crowd. The day before, King Tribhuvan had died while on a state visit to Switzerland, and astrologers had chosen 4:21 p.m. on the day after his death as the most auspicious time for the crowning of his successor, Crown Prince Mahendra.

On the afternoon of the crowning, the cholera hospital cancelled its clinic, and Helen was again front and centre to hear the brass band playing martial music and to watch in awe the pomp and ceremony that rivalled a British coronation at Westminster Abbey. The extravagance seemed incongruous in a country so burdened with poverty and disease.

Later, at the great golden temple of Pashupatinath on the Bagmati River, the king's flower-covered body was prepared for cremation. In accordance with Hindu funeral rites, the oldest son, the new King Mahendra, touched the funeral pyre with a burning torch. He and his two brothers then had to shave their heads, wear only white *dhotis* (loose-fitting cloths tied around their waists) and, for thirteen days, worship, bathe and eat at a temple by the side of the river according to strict rules and traditions.

The death of the king had direct implications for the cholera hospital, at least for two weeks. Government offices closed down for the thirteen days of *kiriya* (Hindu funeral observances), life in the city slowed, and nearly every shop in the bazaar closed its doors. Because the government hospital also closed, the staff of the cholera hospital had to pick up the slack and carry the extra workload.

The beds of the cholera hospital were almost always filled, but not always with sick patients. On a break between clinics one afternoon, Helen walked along the Bagmati with her nursing friend, Becky. They both noticed a forlorn-looking family by the riverside—a homeless mother with two small, pale and sickly looking children. Becky invited them to the hospital for treatment, food and shelter.

The mother slowly recovered from typhoid fever while the children thrived on hearty rice meals and medicine for worms and diarrhea. When the time came for the small family to leave, the eyes of the penniless woman told of the thanks in her heart.

But the end of April approached.

9

Dhar Hospital

It was time for Helen to leave Nepal. For Helen this concluded three months of great challenge, some weeping and much joy. No doctor was available to take over when she returned to India and she wondered if it was right for her to leave. She sent a telegram to her mission headquarters in central India asking to stay on at the hospital a little longer. The reply was a tersely worded telegram: "Proceed to Landour."

And so, with an aching heart, Helen began the first leg of her journey back to India. Jay Story noticed later that this was not the same woman who had left. "Something has happened in your life!" he told her.

Nepal had entered her life—to stay. And she had left a part of herself behind in that needy little country. She was so strongly drawn to Nepal partly because the medical needs were so great and the workers so few. The love and family feeling within the United Mission to Nepal, and the incredibly cheerful and irrepressible people of Nepal, also had something to do with the attraction she felt for that country.

While her hands agreed to work in India, her thoughts were never far from the Himalayan kingdom. The country and its people had captured her heart.

She continued to receive letters from Kathmandu. There was still no doctor to replace her, so impetuous Helen sent a second telegram to mission headquarters at Indore, as to-the-point as the first. "May I return to Nepal?" The answer was a duplicate of the first. "Proceed to Landour."

Returning to Landour meant a return to language study, and to this "doer" it all seemed so academic, so far removed from the real life of sick people. For two months she prepared for the second-year exam in Hindi, and although she passed with high scores on paper, she insisted that "these results sure don't mean that my spoken Hindi is right 84% of the time. I still get lots of snickers and laughs for my blunders and *faux pas*."

After jumping the language hurdle, she was ready to be assigned back to the thirty-five-bed Dhar Hospital, where she would again work by herself. Since she knew from the outset her stay at Dhar would be long-term, this intrepid adventurer took a good look around at the hospital's facilities and services to assess the needs. There were many ways to improve medical service to the patients, but the most obvious deficiency was the lack of an X-ray unit. How could any doctor hope to give proper care to patients with broken bones or tuberculosis or bowel obstruction without any X-ray?

Helen wrote about the need for an X-ray machine in a letter to her friend, Kay Hurlburt, in Lethbridge, Alberta. When Kay read the letter aloud to guests at her supper table, no one listened more intently than seven-year-old Jimmy Atwood.

As soon as she had finished reading, Jimmy began to squirm in his seat. He reached deep into a pocket of his blue jeans and drew out a fistful of precious little-boy objects. From his collection he picked out two coins.

"I've got six cents," he proudly announced.

Clutching the two coins, he marched to the other side of the table and plunked them down in front of Kay.

For a moment no one was able to speak. Then Kay broke the silence.

"Let's do it, Jimmy. Let's get Dr. Helen her X-ray machine. This is all we need to get started."

On faith and a smile, Kay opened a bank account the next morning and made the first deposit of $1.06. Then she started a round of speaking engagements to local groups and churches, beginning with her own, Lethbridge Southminster United Church, always telling the story of Jimmy's two coins.

The "six-cent story" invariably had the effect of filling collection plates to overflowing. More than $1,500 was raised, enough for a portable X-ray machine, and Dhar Hospital's gift from Alberta, Canada, arrived in time for Christmas.

*****

At Dhar Hospital, Helen could not have asked for a finer colleague and friend than Frances Graham. A retired widow who came to Dhar as nursing superintendent, Francis and her husband, Russell, had worked in India together for many years. As an evangelist, Russell had enthusiastically told the Good News in three languages. After his death, Frances returned to Canada to raise her children. There she took a refresher course in nursing to make up for an absence of twenty-five years. She eventually returned to serve in India.

Helen described Frances as "God's gift to me at Dhar," and found her to be a valued colleague and friend with a great sense of humour, a sympathetic ear and a strong shoulder to lean on.

Not all Helen's medical work was carried out in Dhar's sterile hospital setting with Frances nearby. She often made house calls. One night just before Christmas she was called to a midwifery case to the home of Kesar Bai, a sixteen-year-old expecting her first child. She remembers:

We drove in the jeep about sixteen kilometres over a good road, and then another three kilometres over a very bad road with deep ruts. After a five-minute walk, using flashlights to see our way through the darkness of the village, we reached the house and were warmly greeted.

They led me to a room where Kesar was lying. I stooped down, talked to her a bit and then examined her. Then I looked up. To my great surprise, the eyes of a great ox were looking straight at me. I glanced around and counted two oxen, three cows and two little calves.

We were in a stable! The animals were very quiet and didn't bother us, except that the nearest ox nearly knocked the blood pressure apparatus off the table where I had set it.

Suddenly my mind was flooded with this thought: many years ago, in a place like this, Jesus, the Prince of Peace was born.

Kesar's baby wasn't delivered in the stable after all. Helen decided to take her back to the hospital in the jeep. The young mother and baby travelled well, both ways.

Helen grew to love the gentleness, the friendliness and the patience of the Indian people. But she could never quite comprehend the Hindu caste system which held them so firmly in its grip.

Sometimes the caste system created baffling practical problems for her and the staff. The hospital provided special areas for relatives to cook food for the patients, a widespread custom in many parts of Asia. When the rooms were crowded to capactiy, as they often were, there just weren't enough cooking places to go around and arguments developed. The solution seemed simple to Helen. One day she made the decision to ask families to share cooking stoves and space with other families.

It wasn't so simply settled. No Hindus of any caste, except the lowly sweeper, would allow the relative of a Muslim patient to use their space. In turn, the Muslims refused to cook with the sweepers. Members of one caste would not cook with anyone from another. Someone in the beggar class finally agreed to share with the Muslim— but once again he shook his head. In the end he went out and cooked his meal under a tree.

Although Hinduism and the intertwined culture had a strong hold on most people, many loved to hear stories about Jesus Christ and his teachings. Few were prepared to commit their lives to him and risk the consequences.

One Hindu pandit knocked on Helen's door one evening and said he had come "to teach her many things." She listened intently as he told her his beliefs.

"Just as there is spirit in man, there is spirit in animals. To kill man is sin, therefore to kill an animal is a sin. If we do not show mercy to every animal, God will surely punish us. That is why we love and worship the cow which gives us milk. How can we possibly kill the cow to eat the meat?"

Helen listened to the long discourse, by this time quite used to "sacred" cows and bulls that meandered at will over the city streets. Despite Hindu beliefs, she didn't always display patience with sacred animals, especially when they dared to tread on her turf.

Her vegetable garden, flourishing with the abundant rain, had become a tasty delight for wandering bulls. Her arch enemy, a great black sindhi bull, turned up every night. Although the plot was fenced off, visitors tended to forget to close the flimsy gate and the bull had easy access to vegetable feasts. Even with the gate closed, it wasn't difficult for the bull to reach his heart's desire.

For a long time Helen put up with the bull's night-time forays into her garden, until finally the night came when her patience broke. The unpleasant sounds of the bull tearing out and munching merrily on her corn stalks sent her bounding downstairs and out the door. She shone a flashlight into the eyes of the great beast, and after he slowly turned to walk away, she picked up handfuls of rocks to heave at his disappearing rump.

The next morning she asked her gardener if he could think of a way to get rid of the troublesome black bull. In shocked tones, he answered, "Never! He may not belong to anyone, but he is still sacred. We should thank the gods that such an animal has found us worthy to eat our garden!"

The next night, Helen's black nemesis struck again, and despite the gardener's lecture, her attitude hadn't changed. She threw rocks at him again, and every night after that when he dared to make appearances. Never once did she suffer a twinge of conscience at disturbing his peace.

Hindu traditions seemed impenetrable, and not likely to change. But among government leaders, some visionaries saw the need for change.

Prime Minister Nehru visitied the city of Dhar in December, 1956, accompanied by his daughter, Indira Gandhi. Standing among a gathering of thousands at a parade ground just across from the hospital, Helen was able to understand his simple and direct Hindi message. He called for an improvement in the status of women, a breaking down of the caste system and the elimination of tension among the many ethnic groups of the country.

To Helen, it seemed she had heard a proclamation ushering in a new age for India.

*****

In her three years at Dhar, Helen grew and matured as a medical doctor. But perhaps the most precious knowledge she gained was an awareness and acceptance of her own limitations. The volume of work at the hospital was heavy for every staff member, and as the sole doctor, she bore the heaviest burden by far.

A never-ending stream of patients was brought in ox-carts, horse-drawn buggies or hand-propelled vegetable carts. One woman who reached Dhar after travelling forty-eight kilometres on a bus had given birth to her first twin at home; the second was delivered after her arrival at the hospital. Another woman made a long trip to have her seventh child delivered safely. She had lost her first six at birth. Happily, she returned home with a healthy baby girl.

Helen's job was never boring. She treated patients with malaria, smallpox and tuberculosis and then turned to see what she could do for little children who looked like tiny skeletons with dark, sad eyes. She admitted an eight-year-old boy who weighed eleven kilograms (twenty-five pounds), and his sister who, at ten, weighed a mere thirteen kilograms (twenty-eight pounds). She watched with delight as both children thrived at Dhar Hospital, recovering from typhoid and putting solid weight on their scrawny frames.

Helen had been told at medical school that after the first one hundred patients doctors don't worry any more at night about the people under their care. That prediction didn't seem to apply to her— she had already seen thousands of patients by this time, but still she carried their problems home with her.

She admitted a young mother carrying a ten-month old baby with an uncontrollable cough. Fearing the baby would surely die if he continued to cough so violently, Helen gave him a small dose of cough syrup to provide him some relief during the night.

The mother and baby stayed on her mind and she got up during the night to check on how they slept. Everything was quiet as she entered the ward—much too quiet. She walked softly over to the cot where the sleeping mother held her child and shone her flashlight for a close look.

The weary mother slept peacefully, but the baby cradled in her arms was dead.

It was one of the most painful moments in her whole life. She had to wake the young woman and tell her that her baby had died. "I am so sorry," was all she could say. The mother looked down at her son and tightened her arms about the little bundle, but showed no outward grief. Instead she graciously thanked the doctor for trying to help her baby.

But there was no more sleep for Helen that night, nor the next nor the next. She was haunted by the fear that she had caused the baby's death by giving him a cough suppressant. Her conscience screamed accusations at her every single moment for hours on end. She fell on her knees by her bed to ask God's forgiveness, and then felt she had to share her overwhelming remorse with someone else. Although her colleagues reassured her that she had acted in good faith, in her physically and emotionally exhausted state, she could not be consoled.

It was finally one of her senior non-medical missionary colleagues, Dr. Bob Clark in Indore, who understood her feelings of self-recrimination and guilt. He reminded her that anyone who deals with human lives is bound to experience losses and failures. Even if she felt she had made a serious mistake, if God had forgiven her, she should lift up her head and go on. Helen did go on, emerging from this sad experience a more wise, gentle and humble doctor.

Somehow the tragic cases seemed to have a far greater impact than those that went well. When patients did poorly, for whatever reason, she went over every inch of ground searching for something that might help the next patient.

Early one morning a fifteen-year-old pregnant girl was admitted in a precarious condition with severe anaemia, malaria and malnutrition. The day after she arrived she had a miscarriage. She lost only a small amount of blood, but in her weakened condition it was more than she could endure. She died that night, and Helen determined then and there that a blood transfusion service would be set up.

A few months after her arrival at Dhar, Helen took on the responsibility of caring for twenty-five people in a separate home a few miles from the hospital. It was her first intensive experience with leprosy patients.

She immediately developed a special interest in this complex disease that could result in missing fingers and toes, ulcers on the soles of feet, and deformed hands, blindness and misshapen noses. Scorned and shunned by society, leprosy patients were drawn to Jesus and found in Him the comfort, love and acceptance denied them elsewhere.

There was so much to learn—transcending far beyond the bounds of caring for sick patients. She learned how to listen quietly to harsh words and to accept condemning looks from a family when one of their members died. She learned how to react, and not to react, to abusive or unfair comments. She did her level best, and if she failed, for whatever reason, she prayed for self-restraint with the relatives.

Eventually she could say that God allowed her to sympathize with the family in their sorrow, to keep cool and to speak gently.

When her three-year term had passed in the spring of 1958, and it was time for her to move on, the entire staff of Dhar Hospital gathered to say farewell to their doctor-friend. They presented her with a gift and a tribute, written in their best English:

It will be disfiguring truth if we confine your kindness and magnanimity exclusively to us only. The public of Dhar area who had the good fortune to come under your magnetic and benevolent gaze while ailing will ever fondly cherish your memory.

We are numbed by the thought of your going away, but the only silver lining on the dark sheet is the consolation that our sisters and brethren elsewhere would be lucky to avail your noble and selfless service.

The small but well-knit knot of Christian community over here are greatly indebted to you for reinforcing faith in the face of upheavals. You were our guiding star all the time.

Wherever you go, we wish you all the good in the world. May the Lord give you a long, happy and dynamic life to serve humanity.

Helen was moved by these expressions of love and gratitude but equally touching was the gift of a small brass vase from the patients in the leprosy home. Holding it in her hand she realized that these destitute people had contributed from their poverty in order to thank her for her care.

10

Trying So Hard

When it was all over, Helen could look back and say that she was actually thankful, not for the circumstances of one nightmarish week at Hat Piplia, but for what she learned from them.

Following a short holiday after leaving Dhar, she was assigned to work in the village of Hat Piplia for four months. The mission compound consisted of a school, church, a few houses and a small mission hospital that had been without a doctor for more than a year.

Hat Piplia was a colourful village, about twenty-five miles from Indore, full of the kind of vitality that Helen thrived on. On market day, the solitary road was jammed with noisy vendors selling red peppers, peanuts, pumpkins, cotton seed, tobacco, coarse chunks of salt, brightly coloured saris and handmade filigree jewellery. Merchants had to keep one eye on the dark monsoon clouds of the rainy season and another on their wares spread out on the ground.

For the first couple of monsoon weeks, few people came to the hospital. Travelling over the slippery footpaths and muddy roads was dangerous and difficult, and bridges had been washed away by the swollen rivers. The weather improved about the same time as word got around that there was a new doctor in Hat Piplia.

The rains stopped and the flood of patients began. There were so many desperately ill people, young and old, carried or wheeled in overloaded oxcarts to see the doctor. Patients with serious injuries and tropical diseases such as malaria, typhoid and dysentery came in wave after wave.

The heavy workload and the wearisome night calls Helen could manage, but she was not ready for the devastating onslaught of one terrible week when eight patients died under her care.

It was like a baptism of fire. Earlier in the year she had promised to be more obedient to God and to bring every part of her life before Him in prayer, including the care of her patients.

The week reached a climax with the admission of a mother bringing her three-month-old anemic female infant with double pneumonia. Helen warned the mother that it would be a miracle if the infant survived. Then she placed her hands on the baby and prayed for her. By the next day, the baby seemed a little brighter and even playful. With all eyes on her in the open ward, Helen gave thanks to God for the improvement.

The following day the child died.

Helen was devastated. She had built up false hopes for the child's survival and had thanked God when, in effect, He had done nothing. The young mother carried the small bundle in her arms as Helen drove her home in the jeep. She expected to face hard questions and icy looks. Instead, when they reached her home and the mother climbed out of the jeep, she bowed her head before Helen, pressed her palms together oriental style and said softly, "Thank you, doctor, for trying so hard to save my child."

This death, and the mother's acceptance, were almost too much. Inwardly, Helen simmered with anger toward God. Didn't He care about the plight of these frail, sickly human beings? Or didn't He have the power to heal them? Didn't He care about her earnest prayers?

Her week of failures was a fiery ordeal, but it taught her lessons that she never forgot. Her faith in God remained solid, but she came to realize that God cannot be manipulated to fulfill her every wish, even if that wish was for the sake of others. She was sincerely broken-hearted at the deaths, but it dawned on her that some of her anxiety stemmed from a concern for her own reputation. How would all these tragic failures reflect on what people thought of her as a doctor?

A new resolve took hold: she would continue to do her best as a doctor and to trust God. She accepted that suffering and death are an integral part of human experience. Hadn't Jesus suffered undeserved humiliation, torture and excruciating pain before He died?

She set her heart toward learning yet another lesson—to be filled with praise and thanks to God, in times of sorrow as well as joy.

*****

One afternoon Dariya and Sewa, brothers from a nearby village, arrived penniless at Hat Piplia hospital. Dariya had lost most of his vision after an eye infection, and Sewa, not much more than skin and bone, suffered from typhoid and tuberculosis. Their food supply was gone.

Helen gave Sewa food and medication and urged them both to stay at the hospital, but they refused, saying it would be better for Sewa to die at home. She didn't expect to see either of them again, but two weeks later Dariya carried his still-alive brother the six miles back to Hat Piplia. Sewa seemed a little better.

They still had no money, but both needed to stay in the hospital for a considerable time for treatment and decent food. But who would pay for it all?

Helen walked home from work that night, ate her supper and began a letter to her parents dated September 27, 1958.

"Thank you for your most generous gift for my birthday," she began. At the bottom of the last page she casually added a short postscript. "I should like to use your birthday gift to pay for Sewa's treatment and for food for the two brothers. It would bring me great joy. I hope you would agree."

As soon as an Indian lady doctor arrived to take over at Hat Piplia, Helen was freed to accept short-term assignments where the need was greatest. In Ratlam, a city not far from Indore, she worked with a senior missionary doctor, now well known as a former moderator of the United Church in Canada, the late Dr. Bob McClure. After working alone for so long, Helen appreciated having a colleague, especially such an experienced one, to work alongside. She also enjoyed frequent hospitality at Bob and Amy McClure's dinner table.

But she sometimes found herself in disagreement with Dr. McClure's philosophies and actions.

She simply could not accept his policy of withholding treatment from any female tuberculosis patient with two children or more until the woman agreed to a sterilization. But years later, as she looked back and considered India's population dilemma and the immensity of its social and economic problems, she wondered if this harsh policy may have been right after all.

Finally it was time for a vacation, and with missionary friends, the Connors, she travelled to Kathmandu in May, 1957. For the others it may have been purely vacation, but it was a reconnaissance trip for Helen.

She made contact with her old nursing friends Nora Vickers and Becky Grimsrud at their Bhaktapur dispensary and heard for the first time about a new United Mission to Nepal project in the hill country, six days' walk from Kathmandu. Called the Gorkha Project, it had been pioneered only three months before by Jonathan Lindell, a veteran American missionary. Nora and Becky had volunteered as trailblazers for the project and told her they would soon be heading up to live and work at the foot of the mountains of Nepal.

Early one morning near Bhaktapur, Helen took a short hike to pray in full view of these majestic white mountains. As she stilled and quieted her soul, a passage of scripture floated into her consciousness. She heard the visionary words of Psalm 43: "Oh, send forth thy light and thy truth. Let them lead me. Let them lead me to thy holy hill."

11

The Course is Set

Was this call to the hills from God? Was the "holy hill" really the high ridge at Amp Pipal, deep in the hills of Nepal? She had to know for certain. She talked with friends about the new Gorkha Project and prayed fervently, and over and over again the same answer came, softly but clearly. "This is the way. Walk in it."

She started the wheels in motion before returning to Canada for a year's furlough by arranging to meet Jonathan Lindell, who happened to be in Kathmandu gathering supplies. She was certainly welcome to join the Gorkha Project, he told her, but life in the hills would mean isolation, hardships and endless toil. The final decision would have to be made by Mission Council headquarters in India.

Without knowing if she would be returning to India or Nepal, she prepared to leave India. She was ready to go home after almost six years. She had tried to be faithful to the Lord. Although there had been times of great stress and heaviness, she had not been bowed down by it all. In fact, the Connors were to speak of her as "such a caring person and one with a sense of humour, always good fun to be with. She was a 'child of the burning heart' with a deep love for the Lord. And her Christian witness was gracious and spontaneous."

At the end of her first term overseas, her parents received a letter from Herb Ashford, Secretary of the then Missionary and Maintenance Department of the United Church of Canada. Ashford wrote to Will and Edith: *"We are hearing fine reports of Helen, and with her medical skill and her great consecration, she is carrying out a wonderful ministry at Dhar. I am very doubtful if any doctor at any time has lived as definitely in the hearts of the people."*

For six years she had been too busy to feel homesick, but as the ship sailed out of Bombay harbour in May, 1959, she longed desperately to be back in Canada. But what would home be like now? Her parents had moved three times since she had left in 1953. Her sister and two brothers had all married and were pursuing their own careers. Would any of her friends still be around? Would they have changed—even as she had changed?

She met her mother halfway home, at the Mediterranean seaport of Marseilles. Happy to be together, Helen and Edith proceeded on a grand tour that took them to Paris, Italy and over the mountains to Switzerland, where they visited a Bible college in Beatenberg that a friend had once attended. The principal of the Bible college asked Helen to speak before an assembly of students and staff about her own Christian pilgrimage. This assignment presented a dilemma and a new anxiety grew within her. To be truthful, she would have to say that she had accepted Jesus as Lord in India on Palm Sunday, 1954. But tomorrow's audience would include her mother, and to talk about Palm Sunday would imply that her parents had failed to ground her in the faith before she left for India.

Of one thing she was certain: she couldn't sidestep the truth. The next day she stood, tall and poised, before the Swiss students and professors and told them how and when she had reached a point of complete surrender to the Lord. "He is still able to give people new life. He did it for me on Palm Sunday, 1954," she said quietly but with unshakeable calm assurance.

It was the first time Helen's mother had heard this story from her daughter, and it did confuse her, but it wouldn't be the last time, and she would get used to hearing it.

After leaving Europe, and before mother and daughter reached home in Alberta, they had one other stop to make. At Edith's birthplace on Prince Edward Island, which she had not seen for forty-six years, they visited a lifelong friend of Edith. During the course of the conversation, the friend casually remarked, "So Helen, you'll be going to Nepal when you go back."

This was news to Helen—big news. Her mother's friend explained that she had just returned from a United Church Missionary Society meeting at national headquarters in Toronto. The final decision about Helen's appointment had been made at that meeting.

When Jay Story, still back in India, heard the news of Helen's posting to Nepal, he was astounded. As the agent who had started the chain of events that led to her spiritual rebirth, Jay had been following Helen's missionary career with interest. Many years afterwards he wrote: *". . . it surely showed her determination, faith and vision that she dared to tackle the difficulties and to overcome them too. . . . The result was a flood of United Church of Canada missionaries going to serve the people of Nepal. . . . Nepal might have remained a closed country so far as the United Church was concerned if it had not been for Helen Huston."*

*****

Sylvan Lake camp in Alberta had been the scene of Helen's dramatic "on the beach" experience fourteen years earlier, and that summer she attended as camp medical officer, doubling as resident missionary.

One young woman was totally puzzled by Dr. Helen Huston. Jane Loree, a camp counsellor, watched Helen closely. Not only did she not look like Jane's stereotypical image of a "missionary doctor to India," she certainly did not act the part. She always seemed to be where the fun and action were and, in fact, was often the cause of the excitement. As the camp went on, Jane was more convinced than ever that Helen Huston definitely didn't fit the mould.

Jane kept her eye on the tall, energetic woman with the fascinating tales of India and her admiration grew daily. On the day the leaders got into a discussion about what it meant to be a Christian, Jane waited to hear what Helen had to contribute. She was disappointed when

Helen sat and listened without saying a word. Finally someone asked her a direct question and Jane leaned forward to hear her answer.

"When did I first know I was a Christian?" Helen responded with a chuckle. "Not until I was on the mission field in India."

Jane was shocked. If Helen Huston had to go to the mission field in order to really know the Lord, in what kind of spiritual shape was Jane?

The next morning Jane got up very early and walked down to the lake. She sat alone for a long time, in prayer and meditation, and then set out to find the camp doctor. She asked Helen to lead her in a prayer, and that morning she invited Jesus to be the Lord of her life.

Says Jane Loree of that encounter: "Things have never been the same since."

Helen's year at home, largely taken up with a re-introduction to Canadian medicine and a sharpening of her surgical skills at Archer Memorial Hospital in Lamont, Alberta, came to an end before winter. In September, 1960, she boarded a ship in Vancouver to return to the Far East. One of her stops was at Melbourne, Australia, where she was welcomed like a daughter by the family of Howard Barclay, a teacher with the United Mission to Nepal who would soon be joining the team at Amp Pipal.

Howard's mother confided that a group of people in her area had been praying every week for the little country of Nepal since 1916.

Helen tucked that treasure in her heart and took it with her to her new country. She would be the first Canadian missionary ever to work in "the last home of mystery."

12

The Promised Land

Her dream of 1955 had come true. She returned to "the Promised Land," as she called it, at the end of October, 1960, refreshed and renewed after her furlough in Canada. The monsoon rains had ended and the hills were alive with colour. The Himalayas seemed to be wearing their most shining garments as a special welcome for the Canadian doctor.

Snowy, gloriously beautiful mountains rose as a majestic backdrop to the high blue ridges and terraced hills. Yellow fields of ripening mustard contrasted with brilliant green patches of rice and groves of dark green trees.

It was countryside that revealed its surprises in layers, in waves of sensational contrasts, from lowland jungles to the dazzling heights of "the snows"—all in a space less than one quarter the size of the province of Alberta.

Helen joined Kathmandu's chaotic traffic mix of honking cabs, decrepit buses, *tempos* (motorized rickshaws), bicycles and pedestrians. The markets teemed with artisans selling their handicrafts and with men and women who carried huge burdens on their backs or balanced loads of fruit or vegetables from bamboo poles over their shoulders. Cows and goats wandered through the streets. The smells were strong and enticing. In the melee and confusion she heard again the familiar sounds of screech owls, barking dogs and playing children.

From the moment she stepped foot on Nepali soil, Helen was grateful that others had laid the groundwork for her coming. She broke into a brisk and easy stride, heading first for language study, before setting out on trails that had been blazed by adventurers like herself only three years earlier.

The sleeping city of Kathmandu was touched by the soft, grey light of dawn. Three men were striding over the trail that led west out of the city. Foreigners were rarely seen during the mid-fifties, and foreign trekkers or mountaineers invariably set out for Mount Everest toward the northeast.

On this clear morning in November, 1956, Jonathan Lindell and Bob Fleming, both transplanted Americans, were beginning a reconnaissance trip for the new United Mission of Nepal (UMN), a three-year-old interdenominational mission agency established to serve and to work hand in hand with the people of Nepal.

Their Nepali porter accompanied them toward the Gorkha District, high in the roadless hinterland. Bob Fleming, intent on helping the mission, had another project in mind as well. Binoculars slung around his neck and sketchbook in hand, he was in search of the many and varied birds distinctive to Nepal—just as he had done on that first visit to Nepal in 1949.

Jonathan Lindell, a veteran missionary teacher, had already worked for five years with the Nepali people who lived along the India-Nepal border. He knew the country, the culture and the Nepali language and was aware of the great needs of the people living in primitive conditions in rural areas.

It was Jonathan who had conceived the plan to extend the United Mission's work beyond the valley cities to the remote hills. He envisioned a practical, down-to-earth "Community Service Program" to upgrade the quality of life in an especially primitive and needy area in Nepal.

Because education was a major thrust of Jonathan's plan, he sought approval for the project from Nepal's Ministry of Education. At the office of the Education Secretary he explained what he had in mind— to establish a new work in an area not too remote from the capital city of Kathmandu but with virtually no services of any kind.

The Secretary listened to the plan and then turned to survey a map on the wall of his office. He began to write quickly and just as quickly handed over a list of districts which fit Jonathan's "desperately needy" criterion. "Take your pick," he said.

Jonathan looked down at the list and then up at the map, and back again to the list. He had expected more guidance than this. "What about the Gorkha District?" he asked, knowing as little about it as any other place on the list.

"Fine," said the Secretary. "But first you'd better go and see it for yourself."

And so it was west to the Gorkha District that the men were heading this morning. They had a rugged five-day trek ahead of them and would climb a range of hills 1,980 metres above sea level and then descend again to a misty valley floor 1,220 metres down, repeating the climbs and descents over a distance of 128 kilometres. They would have to cross six rivers on shaky suspension bridges and ford other streams on foot.

An estimated 250,000 people lived within the folds of the mountains and valleys in the Gorkha District, which had once had its days of glory.

Looking over the mist-covered valley.

In the eighteenth century, Gorkha Town served as the royal seat for the "Father of Nepal," King Prithvi Narayan Shah, and his court. After the city-states of Nepal were conquered and united under this king, and the capital was moved to Kathmandu, Gorkha declined and never recovered. The king's magnificent palace fell into neglect and eventually ended up as a museum. Gorkha District as a whole changed little in the next two hundred years. It had always been desperately poor.

The district might have dropped into total obscurity but for the renown it gained by giving its name (slightly misspelled) to the Gurkha soldiers. Gurkhas are still known worldwide as "the bravest of the brave." They fought for the British and Indian armies in both world wars and in the 1982 Falklands campaign. It is said that enemies trembled to hear they were facing the fierce fighting regiments from the Gorkha District of Nepal.

Gurkhas have been depicted as "ideal, perfect soldiers." They are described as "having bodies that are short, stocky, muscular and wiry. In disposition they are straightforward, honest, natural, confident and merry. They are absolutely loyal, fearless, and taking to discipline and order. They go into battle, not wildly, but with grim, quiet purposefulness, businesslike. When the enemy is within striking distance, they prefer to go in with their long, curved swords, the khukuri."

The qualities and strengths of the Gurkha soldiers were mirrored in the people who lived in the Gorkha District, although Jonathan and Bob met no fierce villagers brandishing *khukuri* knives when they pitched their tent at Gorkha Town. Early the next morning they puffed their way up Gorkha mountain, reaching the top just after the sun's rays had struck the crags and contours of the great white peaks. In the middle distance rose a series of high ridges and in between, deep valleys still in shadows.

Suddenly Jonathan's wandering gaze was arrested by a curious geographical feature, a pass that resembled a giant saddle between two mountains.

Clearly visible in the morning sunshine, the saddle rose above a broad valley several miles west. "Amp Pipal is the name of that place," their guide informed them. "And the sharp peak on this side of the pass is Lig Lig Mountain."

Said Jonathan, "That's where I'd like to go."

He was far from the impulsive type, but Lig Lig and Amp Pipal were places he just had to explore. At noon the party set off on a downhill walk to the river valley, through knee-high waters of the Daraundi

River, and finally an uphill hike onto the saddle of the curving ridge, a walk that surrounded them with incredible natural beauty.

They reached at Amp Pipal (pronounced 'awmp people') just before dark. At sunrise, the morning beauty was even more breathtaking than the evening sunset. The panorama of hills, valleys and high mountains was accentuated by golden terraces of ripening rice that clung to the slopes, and red splashes of wild poinsettia bushes that stood out like beacons on the hillsides.

The village headman welcomed the strangers and offered to escort them through the village bazaar. Crowds gathered to see their first Western visitors. Jonathan's experienced eyes saw the human pain beneath the surface beauty of the land. If this first walk through Amp Pipal was any indication, then hidden in the villages of these hills and valleys were fathomless pools of human suffering and misery.

In the village homes, filled with smoke, flies and filth, he looked into the eyes of emaciated and malnourished children. It humbled him to meet the gaze of skimpily clad, barefoot adults with deformed limbs and women and young girls bent under incredibly heavy loads of firewood.

Apart from a school for a select few Brahmin boys at Harmi, a village an hour's walk away, no opportunity for education of any kind existed. And there was no health care beyond the craft of herbalists and witch doctors.

The quest was over. For a moment Jonathan closed his eyes on the beauty and the pain. This village, Amp Pipal in Gorkha District, was just the place he had been searching for. He thanked God for the ridge that had caught his attention and led him here.

Now there remained the relatively simple task of obtaining final approval for the project from the Education Ministry which had directed him to the Gorkha District in the first place. Surely that could be easily wrapped up by a quick visit to the government office building at Singha Durbar in Kathmandu.

13

Pioneers in the Hills

On February 20, 1957, Jonathan Lindell held in his hands the Education Ministry's agreement authorizing the Community Service Program in Amp Pipal.

It had taken only seventy visits to various government offices, spread throughout the city of Kathmandu, to obtain this official and final approval!

A few weeks later he was on the upward trail again, leading a group of five to Amp Pipal. The party included Ron Byatt, a school teacher from Britain, Shillingford Mukhia, a Nepali teacher who had previously served with a mission in India, a cook, runner and mailman. Seven porters followed with supplies and chattels.

After five days of hard trekking along the spider's web of timeworn trails, they reached their destination. March 10, 1957, would stand as the historic founding day of the Gorkha Project. The first night, they set up their tent in the village headman's field and cooked their meal of rice and lentils over an open fire.

Early the next morning, the town crier walked up and down the hills, calling on the villagers to gather in the bazaar. The new arrivals were asked to explain to the large crowd why they had come.

In fluent Nepali, Jonathan greeted the people and then outlined the community project plans. Using his visual aid, a blackboard set up in the field, he first drew a schoolhouse to represent education, a dispensary for health care and a field for agriculture. He explained each one of these project aims, and then he drew a fourth picture—a book.

"We have with us a book," he said. "Not an ordinary book, but a book which has in it the words of the creator of the world, the words of God. We would like to share the words of this book with you."

Then, turning again to the large crowd, he asked, "Do you want us to come here to work with you?"

Two days later he received the village's answer. A document four feet long and written in old-fashioned Nepali by a village scribe bore

Amp Pipal villagers greeting the first visitors from the UMN.

the signatures of two village leaders and the thumbprints of fifty-eight others. The sixty elders had unanimously agreed to welcome the mission team, and they promised to cooperate with them as much as they could.

The Gorkha Project had taken its first step exactly the way Jonathan had hoped, by making decisions and progress not for the villagers, but with them.

Now that the project had been given the go-ahead, Jonathan and his colleagues hardly knew where to start. The medical needs and opportunities were, he said, "so vast they could not be measured."

Even so, in one of his first reports to UMN headquarters he wrote,

Jonathan Lindell (with no medical training) and his first patient, a burned baby, deposited in front of his tent.

Beginnings of the first school at Amp Pipal. The boys met under a tree.

"Every day that we can be in this place at our assignment we consider a gift of grace from the Lord."

Four days after arrival they had a base, an ideal piece of property on a flat knoll. The village elders helped arrange the sale for seven hundred rupees (equivalent to seventy Canadian dollars). The missionaries could round up half that sum and a village merchant offered to lend them the remainder.

Two days later, a mother brought her badly burned infant to Amp Pipal and laid him at the door of Jonathan's tent. It didn't seem to matter that they weren't doctors or nurses.

The four blackboard pictures—education, medical work, agriculture and teaching of the Bible—developed into dynamic programs almost simultaneously. School, with Shillingford teaching, started at the foot of a shady tree. The group of twelve boys who gathered every morning for lessons in reading and writing became the first in their medieval society to learn about the world beyond Lig Lig Mountain.

The mission team cultivated a piece of their newly acquired land, planted a garden in the fertile soil, and were soon eating cucumbers, tomatoes, beans and bananas.

The fourth component of the project was considered the most important, for it held all the others together. The team gave thanks to God in a simple outdoor worship service before a group of curious onlookers.

After six weeks the men moved into a temporary home—a shelter framed with split bamboo, plastered with clay and roofed with woven bamboo mats. A stone building would have to wait until the team runner returned with more tools from Kathmandu, because the village owned only an axe and a rough hammer for shaping stones.

It was stressful work and Jonathan missed his family. By the end of six months he had lost sixteen kilograms (thirty-five pounds). Even so, he called it "work with happiness in it."

For Christmas he walked to Kathmandu and, after the holiday, returned to Amp Pipal with his wife, Evey, and three young daughters. He had made a good start on a stone house for his family, on a hillside near the saddle with an expansive view of the valley. It was half-finished, without doors or windows installed, but he considered it luxury after the bamboo shelter.

It didn't strike Evey as all that luxurious, but with ingenuity and good humour she took charge and turned her new home into the hospitality centre for the entire team.

The original Gorkha Project team was joined by two experienced nurses. Becky Grimsrud and Nora Vickers, both friends of Helen Huston, trekked with the Lindells from Kathmandu. Armed with basic medicines and supplies, they were prepared for patients, but they certainly hadn't anticipated being confronted by a steady stream of seriously ill and injured.

The two nurses were the only source of medical care within days of walking and immediately found themselves functioning as both nurses and doctors. They worked out of a flimsy bamboo shelter which was given the grand name of "dispensary." In their first year, they saw sixteen thousand patients. For two and a half years they handled by themselves every kind of medical challenge and emergency, including malaria, typhoid, tuberculosis and leprosy.

Not until November, 1960, was their friend Dr. Helen Huston due to arrive to take charge of the medical work. When an ancient DC-3 of the Royal Nepal Airlines Corporation (R.N.A.C.) lumbered its way down the Kathmandu airstrip and into the skies on November 8, 1960, a new schedule got underway. Now passengers could get to Palangtar in the Gorkha District in forty minutes, a great saving over the old six-day trek. The flight to Palangtar was a new venture for R.N.A.C., and it was equally new—and a bit scary—for one of the passengers, Helen Huston. Although she had read every document and questioned scores of people, it was still like stepping into the unknown.

Sitting beside Becky, who had met her in Kathmandu, Helen leaned her head back against the seat and looked out at the emerald green waters of the Marsyandi River running parallel to the airstrip. She and Becky braced for a landing but were surprised when the pilot pushed open the throttles and began another circuit. They looked out the window at the comical scene of men and boys frantically chasing animals off the landing strip. Palangtar airfield doubled as a grazing ground for cows and buffaloes.

The DC-3 finally landed and Helen stepped out of the aircraft to be instantly surrounded by throngs of people. They had seen airplanes in the sky before but never at close range on the ground. Hardly any of them had even seen a car. The landing near their village was as exciting as a festival.

Helen's heart warmed to these people at first sight. Children and young people outnumbered everyone else—slender and subdued girls with jet black hair parted in the middle and sleekly combed back into braids. She smiled at exuberant boys wearing shorts and, on their heads, distinctive Nepali peaked "topis," and little tots clad only in cotton vests, as excited as young calves.

Becky spotted the two slender, bandy-legged porters who had been sent down the mountain to carry Helen's bags and supplies. One was hardly more than a boy, and neither looked strong enough to carry the medical supplies and all her goods.

Becky sensed Helen's doubts. "Don't worry about them," she reassured her. "And don't interfere when they load up."

Helen watched in amazement as the porters assembled their loads, tying them together with a thin rope and hoisting the massive burden onto their backs. With a *namlo*, a loop of woven rope, they supported the lower part of the load behind and rested the weight of the load on their foreheads.

The porters were ready to go, except for one final and essential detail. Tea time always preceded an arduous trek. From one of two little teashops on the edge of the airstrip, the two porters and the two women were fortified by the strong, sweet, spicy drink of hot tea, served in metal cups that Helen thought could have been just a bit cleaner.

Then the four set off in single file along a narrow ridge between ripening rice fields and then starting the ascent on a well-trodden, centuries-old footpath up and out of the valley. The noisy old DC-3, the connection with Helen's known world, faded out of sight and sound, and the small party of climbers was left alone and in silence.

The twentieth century seemed far removed from this time capsule. On the narrow pathway, they met head-on a procession of long-horned water buffaloes and scrawny cows, herded along by two ragged little boys.

When they reached the village of Thadi Pokhari they stopped for tea again. The hot and strenuous part of the journey was to come. Ahead of them loomed Lig Lig Mountain. Maybe it wasn't Mt. Everest, but to Helen it seemed like a pretty stiff hike up steep paths and stone staircases. The shade of a tree at a *chautara* (resting place) was a welcome sight, especially for the porters who could sit on the stone structure and rest the weight of their loads.

After Thadi Pokhari they climbed for another hour and stopped again at a *chautara* at the edge of a farmer's field. Partly hidden by a clump of trees stood an ochre-coloured house with thatched roof and open porch. Becky explained that people lived all over these hillsides, raising their crops of rice, corn, millet and buckwheat. From here they looked down at the airstrip and the mighty Marsyandi River far below.

It was beginning to get dark before they reached the next village, Borogaon, and although Becky had energy to spare, fatigue was taking its toll on Helen. They pulled out flashlights and slowly continued on a more level pathway. They had been on the trail for four hours.

In the distance, they saw a beam of light bouncing in front of them and getting closer. It wasn't a welcoming party. A young Nepali runner bore a note for the new doctor. She was needed at the dispensary right away for an emergency. There was work to be done and she hadn't even arrived on the scene yet!

They stepped up their pace and within half an hour reached the Amp Pipal ridge. Then they raced down to the dispensary where Nora was attending a young woman in difficult labour. Two hours later, the doctor and the nurses helped the young mother deliver a healthy baby.

Finally Helen was able to sit down to supper. She wondered if the new mother was anywhere near as tired as she was. To keep placing one foot ahead of the other for four and a half hours had been a real endurance test.

She felt a real sense of accomplishment until she remembered that Becky and Nora had both walked six solid days to reach Amp Pipal in 1958. Then they prayed together. Each had something for which to be grateful. Helen's heart simply overflowed with thankfulness for a safe arrival in Amp Pipal.

14

To Work Creatively

In the light of that first morning, Helen surveyed her new home. She stood on the knoll where the first mission house had been built, captivated by the spectacular scenery. She looked toward the north where the giant mountains, the "snows," bore names like Mt. Manaslu, Himal Chuli and Bauddha. Later she learned that Manaslu soared to a height of 8,125 metres, more than two and a half times higher than Cascade Mountain in Banff National Park.

She couldn't remember ever being in a more magnificent spot. The beauty constantly changed before her eyes. In the early morning, clouds in the deep valleys below looked like swirling eddies of water. It was glorious to watch the first rays of the sun striking the peaks with a pinkish glow and gradually turning into a brilliant, glistening white.

The scenery would have to be appreciated in whatever small pockets of time Helen could find, because there was much work to be done.

The nurses had worked out a practical system for dealing with the sick and injured who descended on the dispensary from all directions. In a building that had progressed from a bamboo shelter to a stone-walled, thatch-roofed structure, Helen adapted to the nurses' routine.

The dispensary had no electricity, and the closest it came to running water was the two-legged run of a tiny woman named Thuliko Ama. As an abandoned wife raising children on her own, Thuliko Ama earned her living by carrying water in kerosene tins up the steep hill from the community well to the dispensary. (Today, at seventy-five, she is still the water carrier.)

Patients coming to the dispensary.

The medical work consumed much of Helen's energy and time, but she also concentrated on the absolutely essential task of learning more of the Nepali language. Two teachers at the Amp Pipal school took her under their wing, and she was soon ready for simple communication. She diligently practiced the four *T* sounds, and the four *D* sounds. She discovered that Nepalis have no word for "thank you" and had provided foreigners with the word *dhanyabad* only because they insisted on having a way to say thank you. She learned that there are no direct and firm ways to say "yes" or "no" in Nepali; and curiously, when most Nepalis shake their head, they mean "yes."

Unable to communicate properly, Helen felt hampered in her efforts to help the nurses. Besides, they had already gained so much experience that they could teach her many things. Because it was all so very different from Dhar, she often felt quite inept.

For one thing, many people arrived in the late stages of their disease, often having tried witch doctors and folk medicine practitioners first.

The medical team did its best, often relying on a combination of prayer and medical skills, but some things simply overwhelmed the members.

Nora's ingenuity neatly categorized the bulk of the medical work into files she called "the five Bs"—burns, bear-mauls, babies, birth complications and bowel problems.

What could they do but laugh when patients couldn't afford even a modest charge for the treatment they received, and paid, in lieu of rupees, with oranges and bananas? When the season changed, the medical workers knew it at once, because payment changed overnight to hot red peppers.

It took some time to work out new routines, but eventually the nurses downstairs and the doctor upstairs developed an efficient communication system. They tied a tin can to a rope outside the dispensary windows, placed a scribbled note on diagnosis or treatment inside it, and, with the rope, pulled the can up or down along the wall.

Every day that they were able to work creatively in this stunningly beautiful part of the world, they considered it a gift from God.

*****

After just a few months with the Gorkha Project, Helen felt like she would be deserting the ship by leaving Amp Pipal to go and work elsewhere. But doctors were desperately needed in the UMN's hospitals in Kathmandu and Tansen, and there was only so much a doctor could do in Amp Pipal's primitive dispensary. The nurses had held the fort on their own for a long time and reassured Helen that they could hold out for a while longer.

During her months in Amp Pipal, the plane service to Palangtar had been temporarily suspended. On January 10, 1961, Helen began the six-day trek back to Kathmandu. Her legs had become strong in the few months of hill living and her stride bold and determined. She walked briskly with her porter, starting out early and finishing late every day. They reached Kathmandu in four and a half days.

Entering the Kathmandu Valley again, she was immediately struck by the fast pace of change in the urban area. New buildings were constructed along newly paved roads and foreign aid projects abounded. The Soviet Union had financed the building of a new hospital. China was surveying for a road north to the border, and the Indian government was working on a new east-west highway project.

The little independent country of Nepal had to cope with other invasions too. Refugees were streaming into Nepal from Tibet, the country to the north that had just been annexed by the People's Republic of China. Nepal was struggling to absorb the influx of thousands of needy people.

The United Mission to Nepal had also changed. By 1961, seven years after its modest beginnings, more than one hundred workers from ten countries, representing fifteen Christian denominations and missionary bodies, served in the various projects of the UMN. The most recent valley projects included a high school for girls, a hospital in Bhaktapur, and a nurses' training school.

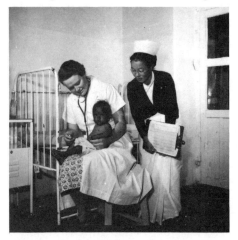

Helen examining child at Shanta Bhawan Hospital, 1961. Rinji, a trusted and capable Nepali nurse, looking on.

The UMN's main medical centre was its one hundred and ten-bed Shanta Bhawan Hospital, a converted Rana palace in Kathmandu. It had taken great ingenuity to fashion a hospital from a palace with a central courtyard, wide staircases and high-ceilinged, rambling rooms. By knocking out walls, erecting partitions and installing fixtures and plumbing, a hospital of sorts was created. The hospital had several wards, an operating room, X-ray and lab facilities and an outpatient department.

It was here that Dr. Helen's skills were needed. She took over the work in obstetrics and gynecology and every week assisted in a few village clinics.

She considered the time at Shanta Bhawan a valuable stepping-stone, "all part of God's plan to give me the experience I need for the hills."

At Shanta Bhawan Helen met Margaret Wright, an American nurse who remembers her as someone who had great difficulty arriving on time for clinics, ward rounds, or, for that matter, anything else. If punctuality was a problem, Margaret says, it was more than made up for by her "gentle and kind way with patients, which endeared her to everyone."

Among Shanta Bhawan's patients during the sixties and seventies were young hippies who flocked to Nepal to "find themselves" and/or to get easily available hashish and marijuana. One of Helen's "flower child" patients had arrived in a pitiful state with hepatitis. The scrawny, dishevelled young American girl was almost penniless the day she came in. Under Helen's care her jaundice gradually improved and she was soon able to walk around.

One day Margaret saw her walking downstairs from the female ward. She blinked at the sight of the skinny girl wearing a set of oversize bright orange flannelette pyjamas.

"Where on earth did you get those fancy pyjamas?" asked Margaret.

"My doctor gave them to me," she said. "I just couldn't stand those horrible hospital gowns."

Later, when it was time for the girl to leave the hospital, Margaret noticed a tear in her eye when she asked her to thank the doctor for loaning her orange pyjamas.

*****

After helping out at Shanta Bhawan, Helen was given another daunting assignment. She was to take over from Dr. Carl Friedericks at the seventy-five-bed hospital under construction in Tansen.

The move provided an opportunity to visit the nine Christians who had been imprisoned in November, 1960. Helen considered it a privilege to make the trip every Sunday to the squalid and filthy prison where she was allowed to speak to them from a distance, standing back one or two metres from the bars.

Months after their arrest, the prisoners told her, they were promised their freedom if they signed a prepared statement renouncing Christianity. Two did sign the statement but were not released. After half a year in jail, they had a visit from a senior police official who accused them of treason for selling out the Nepali people to the Americans. It remains a mystery why this officer considered Christianity the monopoly of Americans.

Finally, all nine prisoners were tried in court and all were found guilty, with sentences to be passed by the end of August. It was not until November, after a full year in jail, that the sentences were handed down. Eight lost their inheritances under the Nepali family system, and shortly after were released. The one who remained behind bars, a pastor who had baptized new believers, was sentenced to six more years in jail.

The harsh treatment of these Christian people might have been expected to discourage the fledgling Nepali church. Curiously, it had the opposite effect of strengthening the believers, and the church grew in number and in faith.

Helen was in Kathmandu for the dedication of the city's first church building. One of the few non-Nepali Christians in the congregation of more than a hundred that Sabbath morning, she joined her voice to songs of praise to God, lifted heavenward in her newly mastered Nepali language.

The congregation gathered in front of the church.

15

Walking Through the Hinterland

After completing her duties at Tansen, Helen and two porters left early one morning for the four-day trek to the lakeside town of Pokhara. She had often hiked over the hills from Tansen to clinics in scattered villages, stopping for tea in the quaint little teashops along the way, sleeping overnight on rice straw mats in thatched houses, and, en route, gaining a deep appreciation for the stamina, wit and hospitality of the friendly Nepali people.

Her trip to Pokhara, recounted in the first person by "the walking doctor," gives a glimpse into the adventure of trekking in Nepal.

As we walked down the mountain, the clouds suddenly opened up, leaving a great blue triangle, with one angle pointing upwards, as if to heaven. At the base of the triangle, the glorious snow range showed through. The sun shone brightly and the whole scene was something of thrilling, overwhelming, uplifting beauty.

A man came running after me for medicine for his eyes. Higher up the hill where we stopped to rest, several older men asked for something for a child with dysentery. A woman at the resting place asked me to read her palm. She had had three sons and three daughters, and all the sons had died.

I try to make it a practice at each stop to look for something new and beautiful. I can't begin to describe all the beauty I saw in leaf, flower, tree, bird and butterfly.

We ate our rice and meat curry lunch by a rushing stream, and then I took off my shoes and socks to soak my feet in the cool water. I gave out some pills for a boy with pneumonia. While we finished lunch, some men ran off to their village to bring back a lady who had a fungus infection on her feet.

The second day was hot, and most of the trail was dry. We met a lady whose relative I had cared for at Shanta Bhawan. She wanted to hear all the news and asked about the Christian prisoners in Tansen.

When we stopped for the night, I slept inside a little house, as close to the door as possible so that I could get fresh air. There were no windows and it was so hot. The folks lit a fire in the corner which temporarily filled the place with smoke. But it was soon out, and the family went upstairs to sleep. I settled down to try to sleep. I jumped about two feet when a dog barked in the doorway. Then the baby upstairs began to cry. Mother began to rock it vigorously and a shower of small bits of clay from the ceiling came raining down on me. The baby settled down and so did I.

Then the fun began. The bedbugs and I played a game of hide and seek. They hid until I closed my eyes and then they sought me. They were getting the better of me until I got up and went after them with a vengeance. I must have killed dozens of them, every one red with my fresh blood. I seemed to be winning, but no sooner did I close my eyes than fresh battalions arrived. After three hours of hard playing, I conceded them the victory and went outside and had a good sleep on the ledge.

Then it was the third morning. We waited until the rains had stopped and set off before noon after our rice meal. This was one of the most beautiful parts of the trek. We walked between fields of rice, usually in ankle-deep irrigation canals, and then through corn that was nine feet high. Women were transplanting rice in muddy fields that had just been *ploughed. Singing as they moved along, they were bent over double and quickly plopped the tender rice seedlings in the mud.*

During the day I counted ten times when we waded through water to our knees. Along the way we met a group of people with a whole lot of questions: "Is Canada east or west of Nepal? (Answer: both.) Is it true that it is dark in Canada when it is daytime in Nepal? How many rupees did it cost you to come here from Canada? How much does rice cost in Canada? Your god, is he the one called Jesus?"

When they asked me if I had come to Nepal to gain merit, I knew they were referring to the Hindu idea of karma. I tried to explain that I had come because my Lord commanded His followers to go into all the world, and to serve others in His name.

On the last day, we set off about six a.m. and hiked back and forth across a winding mountain stream many times as we gained height. I was overjoyed by the great beauty and praised the Lord with all my heart. Then the long trip, mostly downhill, to Pokhara.

Finally reached my friends at the leprosy hospital around seven p.m.— soaked, starving and smelly, but smiling. They treated me royally and I was soon fed, bathed and in bed. No bedbugs! Hurrah!

*****

At the United Mission's annual conference in March, 1963, Helen was officially posted to the Gorkha Project. In November she walked off the plane that had just landed on Palangtar's grassy airstrip and set on the long hike up and around the side of Lig Lig Mountain. She was coming home to the place of her calling. It was a good feeling.

She had company for the walk as far as the village of Borogaon but from there was on her own. As shadows began to lengthen and the sun moved low behind the mountains, she relied upon moonlight that filtered through the clouds. But the light of the moon was eerie, distorting any landmarks she might have recognized in the daylight.

Uncertain of her surroundings, and as fingers of darkness began to press in more tightly, she knew she had lost her way. Nepalis rarely go out after dark, so there was no one to ask the way. At last she saw another person walking toward her and, relieved, she stopped the man to ask directions. The directions were complicated but she tried to follow them, eventually ending up more lost than ever. She realized just how far she was from her destination when she reached the old abandoned fort near the top of Lig Lig, a landmark far from Amp Pipal village.

Dogs howled in the lonely black night, and strange sounds echoed off the slopes. She shivered and kept on moving. Near the village of Maibel an old man approached her on the trail and it was like seeing an angel. He offered not only to direct her, but to lead her wherever she wanted to go, and together they headed down to Amp Pipal. When they reached the familiar cluster of houses, she thanked her elderly shepherd heartily and watched him walk back into the night.

The Amp Pipal nurses had been waiting up for her but had finally given up and gone to bed. They were wakened from their sleep by the sound of Helen singing her favourite hymn, "Praise my soul, the King of Heaven!" Exhaustion could not stop her from singing and giving thanks.

She was "home," and standing on the threshold of a new era. In years to come a unique little hospital would take shape within sight of the mighty mountains: a hospital that would eventually need five doctors and a staff of seventy-five; a hospital striving to meet the needs for health care of nearly half a million people; a hospital that would be the subject of many an article and story; a hospital that would be visited by innumerable people from countries far across the seas.

But that night, there was just a lonely Canadian-born doctor coming home to Amp Pipal.

And as it always does, it felt right to be home. That first homecoming morning, from the tiny window of her new "office," Helen looked out on a spectacular landscape of great trees and ridges of green hills. The beauty was all outside. The inside of the homely two-storeyed, mud-floored dispensary bore little resemblance to the facilities of Shanta Bhawan and Tansen Hospitals.

Nothing much had changed since her earlier visit to Amp Pipal. The sole concession to the growing numbers of patients was made after her arrival. The nurses moved their residence from the dispensary's upstairs floor, freeing the space for conversion to the doctor's examining room, a storeroom for drugs, and an operating room which doubled as lunchroom and tripled as medical library.

Early every morning, patients lined up for preliminary examinations by the nurses on the ground floor. If patients needed the doctor's attention, they either walked or were carried around the corner, up the hill and across a short wooden bridge to the door of the second storey, where Helen examined each one.

For five years the nurses had used the plain and primitive dispensary building as a combined clinic/hospital. Most days found them working until after nightfall, doing what they could to stem the growing tide of suffering and misery. Helen doubted if she was of the same stuff as they.

The Amp Pipal dispensary. Built in 1958, for eleven years it served thousands in the Gorkha District.

At the end of the day Helen would walk to the quaint little Nepali-type home which she and her colleague of Shanta Bhawan days, Margaret Wright, found most satisfactory. Helen considered the floor "good red mud, just like the soil in Prince Edward Island." The smooth red mud floors were perfectly acceptable to Helen and Margaret for a long time, until the rats burrowed under the wall and suddenly appeared in the middle of their living-room. Their next requisition form for mission supplies included an urgent order for a few bags of cement.

At ground level, rats ate anything and everything that wasn't ingeniously stored, and many things that were. They were as much a problem as the insects, that incessantly chewed away at the thatched roof. When the rains of the monsoon season found the cracks, the two women slept with open umbrellas perched by their heads.

A few months after her arrival, Helen was officially appointed as medical superintendent of the Gorkha Project, and by April, Ron Byatt, assistant to Jonathan, wrote to UMN headquarters that she had settled in so easily "it seems as if she's always been here."

Nora, one of the pioneering nurses, wrote to Helen's parents, *"What a tremendous load of responsibility her coming has lifted from Becky and me professionally. And what a load of joy it has brought to us personally!"*

Nora admired Helen's capacity to accept the limitations of medical facilities and supplies, and admitted, "On this mountaintop, about the only thing we're never short of is sick and injured people."

When the burden of work grew too heavy, the medical workers would join other members of the mission team and, with packed picnic lunches, hike up the slopes of Lig Lig. From the heights they could look down and across to the collection of unimpressive buildings—and gain some perspective on the scene that so monopolized their lives. It was really no more than a miniscule island in a broad sea of green terraced hills and white mountains.

16

Much Laughter and Sometimes Tears

Along with medical experience and a capacity to work long and hard, Helen brought laughter and singing to the Amp Pipal dispensary. Her friends and co-workers liked to bait her just to hear her delightful laugh.

Nurse Val Collett had just completed a visit to the patients staying in the *deras* (a small, simple shelter for six patients) when she met Dr. Helen on the pathway. Clicking her heels in mock military fashion, she said, "Doctor, I'm here to report on the patients in the *deras*."

Helen played along. "Yes and have you anything interesting to report?"

"I do," answered Val. "The patients are all getting better, and all six have the same disease."

Helen raised her eyebrows. "All the same disease?"

"Yes, doctor. All bites. Two were mauled and bitten by a bear. Two are recovering from leopard bites. And one was attacked by a monkey and bitten on the leg."

"But that's only five and I know all six of the *dera* beds are full."

Val chuckled. "Believe it or not, the sixth one is a bite too—but just a little different from the others. This patient was bitten by her husband's other wife. Hers is the bite that hurts most of all!"

Sometimes it was the spontaneity and ingenuity of the village people that provided comic relief, and sometimes it was a simple thing like a *patooka*. Helen was not a great fan of the *patooka*. As a foundation garment worn over the clothes of Nepali women, it consisted of several yards of material wrapped round and round the waist, and in the crevices and folds women stored coins, cigarettes, vegetables and even baby chicks.

Helen regarded *patookas* as a nuisance that was restrictive and impractical. It took too long for a female patient to unravel layer after layer of material before a medical examination.

She changed her mind about *patookas* when one came to the rescue of a woman who had just had abdominal surgery. There were post-operative complications and her wound took a long time to heal. The weakened tissues allowed a huge swelling to develop at the site of the incision, but this mother of three small children had no time to recuperate.

She left for home and returned for her checkup a month later. Dr. Helen marvelled that she had gained weight and was clearly making a good recovery. She asked the woman about the big bulge and whether it was causing her any trouble.

"Oh no," she replied, "in the morning before I get up to feed the buffalo, I just wrap my *patooka* tightly around me."

The lowly *patooka*, Helen had to admit, made a pretty fine surgical corset!

Sometimes, when the dispensary staff felt like crying, singing helped. As they unwrapped the dressings on the burn wounds of a little girl named Saraswati they sang her a simple tune:

"Saraswati, Saraswati,
Kati ramro, nani ho."

Roughly translated, they were singing, "What a good little girl is Saraswati."

Only four years old, Saraswati whimpered ever so slightly as the nurses changed dressings on the painful burns on her legs and tummy. Time and gentle care healed Saraswati's wounds, enough for Helen to cover them with skin grafts. She sent this little girl home with nearly all her burns healed and with the Saraswati song forever etched in her memory.

The songs and laughter were a lifeline. Beth Brunnemaier, an American nurse who joined the dispensary team for three years "in the early days," recalls that Helen saw "literally multitudes of patients."

Beth described the daily scene of patients waiting at the dispensary. "So many were ghastly, hopeless, serious, complicated, filthy, persistent, desperate people. Helen and the nurses worked from twelve to fourteen hours daily, and often into the night."

Sometimes they couldn't keep up. A young mother was carried to the clinic one morning, severly dehydrated from vomiting and diarrhea. Helen immediately started to give intravenous fluid to the haggard and listless patient and placed her on a *gundri* (rice straw mat) on the dispensary veranda. Then she ran off to start the busy clinic, intending to come back shortly.

But a couple of hours passed before she could get away. She rushed to the veranda but it was too late—her patient had died.

Could she have been saved? Should Helen have stayed behind, ignoring the others with their pressing needs, and given her full attention to this critically ill patient? Perhaps, and henceforth she resolved to pray for the wisdom and judgement needed to determine who needed priorty care and who did not.

During three years in Amp Pipal, Beth said, ". . . The laughs and jokes and ridiculous happenings eased the seriousness of the case load. . . . During the three years I was there I never once heard a (complaining) sigh or a groan but I sometimes saw tears of stress.

". . . at times we would stop for prayer in the middle of rounds or for praise—especially when a patient with bowel obstruction began to pass wind!"

At least one of the Gorkha Project nurses had at first greeted Dr. Helen's coming to Amp Pipal with apprehension. Nora feared that the situation would be too difficult for a single doctor to handle. The nurses were established and well known to the communities, and despite constant reminders to their patients that they were "just nurses," the local people couldn't be convinced. They called them the "old doctors."

As "charter members" of the Gorkha medical work, these nurses were also rather settled in their routines. When the doctor came, would they have to change everything familiar? Would their simple ways and limited equipment be an intolerable frustration for a medical doctor who was accustomed to so much more?

Nora's fears didn't materialize. "God sent us a doctor," she marvelled, "with a great capacity to draw on His grace, and one with whom we had a warm, personal friendship." Although the nurses' role became a supportive one, from the outset Nora, Becky and Helen formed "a team without a hierarchy."

The little team of health care workers had no spare time to worry about status. On a routine day they prepared to see one hundred patients, and on a heavy day, many more. They handled tuberculosis, hookworm anemia, scabies, dysentery and typhoid, and just assumed everybody had worms ("including ourselves," someone said).

The "routine" ailments they could handle. But when a crisis situation came along, they longed for a hospital, and it was a rare day when the dispensary routine wasn't interrupted by an emergency.

Early one Monday morning Helen and the nurses had just completed the rounds of their "in-patients." Already ninety people had registered for the day's clinic and were patiently waiting to be seen. Some had walked three days to reach the dispensary and many had slept outside overnight.

All at once a commotion ruffled the crowd outside the dispensary. People shifted to the side to clear the way for two men who carried a woman on a *doli* (a sort of hammock slung under a pole). Panting, the men put their burden down at the door.

Dr. Helen was called outside, and she crouched on one knee at the side of a young woman in her thirties. The men said she had been in labour for three days. Helen drew back the folds of covers, revealing a thin, pinched face and sunken eyes and cheeks. The woman's abdomen was hard and tender all over. Helen felt her pulse, weak and thready, and listened for the baby's heartbeat, but heard nothing.

After three days of obstructed labour the uterus had ruptured and the baby had died. The mother was *in extremis*, close to the end. There was still a thread of hope, but Helen had never done the operation that could save the woman's life.

She started an intravenous of a blood substitute to sustain the woman until she could crossmatch blood from the relatives. Then, holding the woman's limp hand, she asked the Lord to guide her through the operation. The message came clearly: get on with the job.

The entire staff prepared for the operation. Simple facilities and a primitive setting did not stop them from aiming for proper cleanliness and sterilization. Everyone helped except Jagat, the Nepali records clerk who tried to pacify all the disappointed waiting patients.

It was a crisis moment, but Helen felt she was not in it alone. After the patient was put to sleep, she opened the abdomen, removed the dead baby and repaired the ruptured uterus.

Afterwards, the patient's condition slowly improved and she went on to survive the ordeal. The staff thanked God for guiding the hands and mind of the new Amp Pipal doctor.

As for Helen, after closing up the incision, she collapsed, exhausted. But it was what Jonathan Lindell would have called "happy fatigue."

17

Flickering Lights and Fireballs

Mary Varghese found it reassuring to have Dr. Helen nearby the night she went into labour with her third child. The wife of Thomas, the Indian headmaster of the mission school in the village of Luitel, Mary was having strong pains but not making progress.

Hour after hour passed, and Helen saw signs of fatigue in her friend. "Mary," she said gently, "the baby's head is still riding high, and I'm getting a bit worried because the pulse is slowing." She stayed close by during another hour of strong contractions that failed to make progress, and then decided on the course of action that would save both mother and baby.

"We must operate, dear friend," she said. "I've already explained everything to Thomas. I'll ask the nurses to get everything ready."

The generator wasn't working—again—so the nurses dusted off and lit the old kerosene pressure lamp. They prayed together before Mary moved over to the wooden operating table. It would be tricky surgery because the nurse giving anesthesia had to go easy with the ether in order not to depress an already stressed baby.

Moths flew around the lamp. Its erratic flickering barely gave off enough light for Helen to see where to make the incision for the Caesarean section. The baby was so large (four kilograms, or nine pounds) that she had to struggle to deliver it.

Eventually she succeeded, and when the newborn infant took his first breath and cried, there were cheers and tears. Mother and baby did well, and later the child was christened Aanand (Nepali for "joy").

A few years afterwards Aanand would be told the story of his birth. Later, he graduated from high school and subsequently travelled to the U.S.A. for university.

Mary Varghese and her newborn son soon returned home leaving the dispensary staff wondering when to expect the next "dramatic episode." They did not have long to wait.

It happened during a bizarre "dry season" storm that unleashed violent elements of nature upon the Amp Pipal ridge.

It was pitch-dark and a gale was howling through the trees, threatening to whisk off every thatched roof in the village. White-hot forks and sheets of lightning tore the sky open, and black clouds swirled into convulsions. Ear-splitting roars of thunder shook the mountainside, and driving rain sent murky water surging and cascading in rivulets down the rough village "street."

On the upper floor of the dispensary, in an area grandly designated "operating room," the medical team was gathered around the operating table. On it lay a young man who had been fit and healthy that morning, but during the day had fallen from the edge of a cliff and suffered serious injuries.

Nurse Becky Grimsrud was circulating. Val Collett, a slender nurse from England, had put the patient to sleep with open drop ether and, with ether fumes filling the room, was beginning to feel somewhat anesthetized herself.

Helen tried to visualize what an X-ray would show of his fractures. She made her decision and shouted above the noise of the storm to her operating room assistants.

"I'll reduce the fractured humerus [upper arm] first and put it in plaster. The toughest job will be wiring his broken jaw."

The three worked steadily in what could at best be described as sub-optimal conditions. At least the generator was going again. Perhaps it did function erratically but when it worked, light from the one bulb was sheer luxury. How they appreciated Herman Simrose, the agricultural worker from Moose Jaw, who had run a power line from his workshop to the dispensary.

The broken arm was reduced and a plaster cast applied before Helen turned her attention to the young man's face. Fragments of his broken lower jaw were sticking into his mouth.

This was a case of any treatment being better than nothing. Helen could straighten his jaw all right, but she'd have to wire his teeth together to hold it straight.

The task of inter-dental wiring was well underway when a virtual bomb-blast of thunder ripped the night apart. The operating room was left in total darkness.

They hadn't seen it, but a glowing red fireball had shot like lightning through the electric lines from Herman's workshop to the dispensary and other mission buildings. It had blown out all the wiring.

Becky left the operating room to go downstairs in search of a flashlight or candle. Feeling her way through the darkness and along the stairs, she was almost at ground level when she smelled smoke. Then she spied a ruddy glow across the room, in a far corner. A grass broom that leaned against the electric wiring was smouldering and about to burst into flames.

Becky quickly doused the broom in a pail of water, grabbed a flashlight, and ran back upstairs to the waiting operating room staff to tell them what she had found.

"If you hadn't gone downstairs to get a light, my dear, the whole building would probably be in flames now," said Val.

In the darkness they took time to give thanks to the Lord who once again had protected them from danger.

During it all the patient slept soundly, thanks to the old-fashioned reliable ether. With the help of the flashlight, Helen inserted the last wires between his teeth and then wired both jaws together, thus securing the broken fragments.

Early next morning they looked in on their young patient with the wired-together jaws; he was doing just fine. A few weeks later Helen removed the wires and he was soon back to eating his twice-daily rice.

Outside the old dispensary, where Helen is overseeing some patients.

18

Friends from Far and Near

In 1965 Helen's life was enriched by two kindred spirits who arrived at Amp Pipal. Asbjorn and Mia Voreland came from Norway with their three young daughters, Asbjorn to teach at the school and later to take on responsibility as project director.

Mia provided priceless gifts of kindness and encouragement that often lifted the spirits of Helen and the nurses. The Vorelands still live and work in Nepal, and Mia looks back fondly on those early days at Amp Pipal when the medical team often finished work and came to her home long after dark:

"Sometimes we would invite them for supper, throwing together what we could find. The girls were so happy to have a meal with a family after a long day with medical and staff problems. It was fun to see how they revived after food! . . . I'll never forget the times of sharing the Word around the table; the deep fellowship in sharing and praying bound us together."

With open hearts and arms, the mission team also welcomed Nepali helpers. The Gorkha Project was a grass-roots venture, a "working with the people," as Jonathan had promised from day one.

It was certainly clear from the size of the workload that more hands were needed to help with the daily onslaught on Amp Pipal's dispensary.

One of the first Nepali helpers was a former patient from Shanta Bhawan Hospital. Shyam Krishna Ranjit recovered from rheumatic fever and then took training as a lab technician before coming to Amp Pipal.

A young Nepali Christian, Ratan, took a short course at a mission hospital in India and was able to change dressings and look after wounds.

Naomi was a tall, soft-spoken Nepali girl, highly valued by Helen for her outstanding service as an assistant nurse. Perhaps her dedication had grown out of suffering. A marriage had been arranged by her parents when she was still a teenager, but unknown to her, her husband already had a wife. What he wanted from a second wife was free labour as a household servant.

Naomi endured a life of degradation for five years, seething with bitterness and resentment, until she became a Christian. After asking forgiveness for her hateful attitude toward her husband and in-laws, she left their home to attend a Nepali Bible school. Following two years of study, she arrived at Amp Pipal dispensary to assist the nurses.

The mission workers were a fine, loyal and hard-working team that Helen described as "a happy group with really very little tension." But incidents of dishonesty and immorality among some of the Nepali workers caused much pain and disappointment, especially if those involved happened to be Christians. They wrestled with the problem of dealing in fairness with otherwise diligent co-workers whose cultural standards and ideals clashed with their own.

Helen never did develop a thick skin about these kinds of problems. As if they were her own children, she grieved for every staff member who broke trust in action or attitude.

If she felt herself growing discouraged by the behaviour of a few Nepali colleagues, her hope was renewed by simply reminding herself of Jagat. To this day, she considers him one of the most remarkable and trustworthy of all the colleagues she has ever worked with in any country.

It was a miracle that Jagat was even alive. Before Helen's arrival at Amp Pipal, in 1961, he was carried in a *doli* to the dispensary with advanced tuberculosis of the lungs. He was given a place in the *deras* and the nurses started him on treatment, although his wife, Jagat Maya, was certain that he had reached the end of his earthly trek.

For two nights Jagat coughed up blood, and on the third night he lapsed into a coma. Jagat Maya ran down the hill through the trees to find a nurse. It was 3:00 a.m. but Nora got up and raced back with her and gave him an injection. Nora stayed with him during the night, and resting his head on her lap, she prayed. Jagat awakened enough to hear her prayers, but her voice seemed far away.

He improved slowly, but the battle wasn't over yet. On three occasions he was hit by pneumothorax (air leaking out of the lungs into the chest cavity). Each time the nurses had to insert a needle between his ribs to allow the air to escape. As he fought to live and made steady progress toward recovery, Jagat was deeply moved by the love and care he received from the Christian nurses, especially Nora and Ratan. Slowly and deliberately, he turned his heart toward Jesus, the source of their love and care. Some time later, after watching the remarkable change in her husband's life, physically and spiritually, Jagat Maya joined him as a new Christian.

For the next four months, while still a patient gaining strength in the *deras*, Jagat worked as a volunteer, at first washing out soiled bandages for re-use and then making small pill containers out of old newspaper. When his health continued to improve, he was given the job of registering patients—recording the name of each patient and trying to control the daily patient flow. (Helen preferred to call it a stampede). In later years he was promoted to cashier and general adviser/counselor and public relations spokesman for the mission.

Two years after starting volunteer work, Jagat was faced with the most tearing decision of his life when his father died. As the eldest son in his family, it was his duty to light the funeral pyre. He had loved and respected his father, but to take part in *kiriya*, the Hindu ceremony for funeral rites, would be a betrayal of his new faith. His stand for Christ clashed head-on with tradition, but Jagat stood his ground. He told his family he could not take part.

Word of his refusal spread like wildfire and neighbours gathered in front of his house, shouting at him, "Don't you care what happens to your father? Didn't you love him? Why won't you do his funeral rites?"

The matter was reported, and authorities from four *panchayats* (local governments) met to determine how Jagat should be punished. Some argued that he should be sent to prison for six years. Others felt his whole family should be imprisoned with him. In some ways even worse, many suggested that he should be completely cut off from village life.

Police officers were sent to his house to arrest him but he was at work in the dispensary up the hill. The officers sent his young daughter to deliver a message that he must come home immediately. As soon as he read the message, he started out from the dispensary, but first made a short detour to the Amp Pipal school where a mission convention happened to be meeting. He asked them to pray before heading out the meet the officers.

The short detour set Jagat on a slightly different pathway down to his home, while the police officers took the main path up to the dispensary, expecting their paths to cross. When they reached the top and heard Jagat had gone down, the tired officers returned to their station.

Amazingly, the police officers never did return and he was not prosecuted, nor was he ostracized by the villagers. His Hindu mother refused to disinherit him, and when neighbours urged her to deny him entry to her house, she answered, "Jagat is my son and he can come to my home whenever he wants."

Jagat's reputation for integrity had kept him from being made an outcast in his village. As a legacy from his tuberculosis, he still had trouble breathing and needed help with heavy work. Soon after the controversy died down, several of his Hindu friends carried timber to his land and helped him build a solid thatched-roofed, mud-floored house in Amp Pipal.

Its second owner in 1983 would be a tall Canadian doctor who found it perfect for her needs, except for one thing: she kept hitting her head in the doorway!

19

Dispensary Adventures: From Charles I to the Raw Rice Test

For a long while, no one could remember his real name, so took to calling him Charlie.Of all the cases that puzzled or challenged the medical team, none could quite match Charlie.

Charlie lived in a village three hours' walk from Amp Pipal. One day he fell from a height and landed straddling a sharp stump. He appeared at the dispensary with tremendous bruising and swelling of the crotch area, unable to pass urine and in severe pain. An examination showed that he had ruptured his urethra.

Quaking in her boots, Helen admitted to Val that this was uncharted territory for her. In her surgical training she'd had hardly any experience in urology—had certainly never seen an injury like this.

Val understood and nodded. "We do have catheters and could try to drain his bladder so that he wouldn't have so much pain."

"I don't think a catheter would be enough," said Helen. "Let's get out the book and see what else we can do."

Together the doctor and nurse located an old textbook on urology in the upstairs library, turned to the chapter describing urethral injuries and eagerly read on. It looked like an awesome undertaking, but there was really no choice; the man would certainly die if not treated. They went ahead and prepared for the operation.

Val put the patient to sleep with ether and then read the book aloud to Helen. First Helen drained the bladder through an abdominal incision, then, with much difficulty, passed a catheter from above. Finally she made an incision in the crotch area and found and repaired the torn urethra. It would have been tricky surgery even in a sterile, steel-and-glass hospital.

Charlie made a good recovery. Apart from one day when he suddenly passed a lot of blood-tinged urine, he made slow but steady progress. In due course all catheters were removed and he was able to pass urine on his own. It was time for much rejoicing.

But Helen knew from Bob McClure's teaching that the job was incomplete—the repaired urethra would need dilating or stretching in order to prevent a "stricture" developing. Twenty years later Charlie was still coming back for yearly dilating.

Charlie learned to read and became familiar with the gospels, although he never professed to become a Christian. His son became a teacher in the mission school in Luitel.

In a sense, "Charles I" established a sort of dynasty. Whenever a patient with a "waterworks" problem appeared on the scene, someone would call out, "Come and meet Charlie's brother" or "Charlie's sister" or even "Charlie's aunt."

*****

There was more activity around and about the little dispensary than anywhere else in Amp Pipal village. But activity didn't generate funds, and although woollen bandages and medical instruments were donated, mainly from Canada, there were ongoing costs of drugs and supplies, as well as salaries for the Nepali staff.

Like most missionary doctors, Helen took little interest in the economics of medicine. But she realized that, in principle, patients should be encouraged to pay something for their care, if only the equivalent of twenty-five to thirty cents. One in every four patients received medical care free of charge. But sometimes the very poor insisted on paying.

Becky remembered the time an adult man and his child, both severely burned, came to the dispensary and were put up in the *deras*. Helen treated them for extensive third degree burns of the face, neck and hands. For a few days they seemed to be progressing, but then they both got tetanus and died on the same day.

The following morning, the man's elderly father came to the dispensary.

"I'll never forget the look of pain in Helen's eyes when the old man reached into his pocket for a few small coins." declared Becky. The best he could manage, he handed the coins over to the doctor who had done her best to help his son and grandson.

*****

The Canadian cardiologist who had long ago told Helen she could live with her heart condition had been right. Fluttering heartbeat wasn't a serious condition, and since her teen years it had given her trouble only occasionally. The medical term, paroxysmal auricular tachycardia, she shortened to "PAT."

Ordinarily, when her heart suddenly began to beat very quickly, making her feel weak and nauseous, she could rely upon pressure over a certain point in her neck to slow her pulse down.

One hectic Monday morning, with 120 patients clamouring to be examined, Helen's old friend PAT suddenly intruded on the scene. She tried to stop it by applying pressure over the carotid vessels in her neck, but felt faint and had to sit down. Then she remembered having brought back from furlough a sample of a new drug that was supposed to be effective against fluttering heartbeat.

A nurse found the drug in the medicine cupboard and read the directions quickly—in fact, too quickly. The drug had to be given slowly by intravenous, but she drew up the dosage in the syringe and gave her colleague an injection.

Helen lay down in the upstairs room of the dispensary, where she was suddenly hit by sickening nausea and a fearful, throbbing headache. She was unable to lie still an instant, and everything looked blurred and out of focus.

The nurses re-read the directions on the bottle of medicine and discovered to their horror that Helen had received ten times the recommended dosage! They took her blood pressure. It was 285/185, a level so dangerously high that her life was at risk from a stroke or heart attack.

Helen credits the prayers offered then and there by the nurses and staff with protecting her life. Later in the day, after the headache and nausea had subsided somewhat, she walked home slowly.

If there was any blame to be laid for the serious error, the culprits were "haste" and "all those patients." Together they pledged that care and caution would not be sacrificed again, despite all the waiting patients.

*****

It started on a small scale, almost imperceptibly. First a transistor radio disappeared, then a small sum of money, then a larger sum. The losses caused some distress to the mission team at Amp Pipal, but no real alarm. But then the problem escalated. Thefts came closer together and more valuable items—a tape recorder and medical instruments, including Helen's ophthalmoscope—disappeared.

The mission finally reported the string of thefts to the local *panchayat*. After hearing the details, they concluded it was probably an inside job. They shared with Howard Barclay, the project director at the time, their special strategy for apprehending criminals.

The head of the local governing body, the *pradhan panch*, told Howard, "Before your church service tomorrow, I want everyone working with the mission to come down to the village. We have ways to find out who is the guilty party."

"How will you do that?" Howard asked.

The *pradhan panch* raised himself to his full height and stuck out his chest. "It's very simple," he said. "We'll give everyone an equal amount of dry, uncooked rice to eat, just enough to cover a one-rupee coin. There will be no problem identifying the thief, because he will start coughing up blood right away."

Taken aback by this interesting style of justice, Howard left the *pradhan panch*, tentatively agreeing to the raw rice test but desperately hoping for a way out. Late at night and still wide awake thinking about tomorrow, he jumped to his feet in an instant to answer the ring of the newly installed party-line phone.

The call was from Sodemba, one of the teachers at the school. "Hello, Howard," he said. "I'm in the farmhouse. We've caught the thief!"

Howard grabbed a flashlight and dashed out into the darkness. At the farmhouse, Howard met Sodemba with his apprehended thief, a slender fourteen-year-old boy who worked in the house of another teacher. The boy admitted to the thefts and offered to return the stolen items and to make retribution.

Satisfied with the turn of events, Howard and Sodema considered the case closed.

But the next morning, as requested, all mission workers appeared in the village "on parade," ready to submit to the raw rice detection test. Howard produced the culprit, who admitted his guilt publicly.

Just at that moment, five policemen arrived on the scene. Summoned by the *pradhan panch*, they had walked for two hours from headquarters at Tadhi Pokhari at the foot of Lig Lig. Howard explained that the thief had been caught during the night and had confessed and offered to work for a few months without wages to make up for the losses.

"We won't lay any charges against him," said Howard.

But the police officers had come too long a distance to let the guilty one off so easily. Justice had to be done and the guilty party punished. They sat with the *panchayat* members, weighing the pros and cons, considering the alternatives, and debating the case at great length.

Hour after weary hour passed while the boy's fate was deliberated, and observers waited patiently. Eventually, it seemed that they were nearing a consensus—the boy would have to be taken to police headquarters in Gorkha Town—and then they renewed debate on this decision.

But it was not to be!

Throughout the entire process, Martha Mukhia, a language teacher and the wife of Shillingford, had been sitting quietly at the edge of the crowd beside the accused boy, whom everyone was ignoring. Martha, blessed with an abundance of wit and humour, saw a solution to the problem.

She turned to the boy and said in her quietest whisper, "*Bhag*," the

Nepali command to "Take off!" In an instant he slithered down the hill and out of sight.

An hour later, the authorities announced, with conviction and solemnity, that they were ready to escort the prisoner to Gorkha Town.

Alas, it was all in vain—the prisoner had vanished!

But no one seemed to mind. It had been an entertaining day. And now it was time to go on home.

Two days later the boy returned to make good his promise to work for the mission. He stayed at the job for three months and worked off much of his debt before joining the army. His life took an abrupt turn for the good, and in her 1967 Christmas letter Helen wrote about "the apparent good-for-nothing thief . . . who recognized and received the Pearl of great price."

*****

The soggy, drizzly monsoon season is hardly the best time to plan a long trip over Nepal's ancient and hilly footpaths. Slippery red mud paths and swollen rivers that have to be crossed on foot are perilous hazards. Leeches that drop silently from leaves and shrubs and then proceed to suck the blood of a passer-by are good reasons to stay at home.

But Helen had a paramount purpose for starting out during the monsoon season on a hike to Barpak. A village of five thousand people, located at an altitude of 2,438 metres at the foot of the snowy peaks, Barpak had no medical care of any kind. The UMN had asked for government permission to open a dispensary in Barpak, but they had been refused.

A few Barpak villagers made it to the Amp Pipal dispensary, but most injuries and illnesses went untreated. Helen knew that a two-day clinic was hardly the answer, but it was better than nothing.

She also had another reason for setting out for Barpak. A handful of Christians from the community had visited the Gorkha Project the year before, and prior to leaving for home had asked if someone from the mission could come to their village a couple of times annually.

The strenuous hilly trek would take two days each way. The umbrella-carrying entourage accompanying Helen included Naomi, the Nepali nurse-aid, Jim Miller, an American builder, and two carriers. Helen kept a record of the fascinating adventure.

Day 1: All the walking involved much climbing up and much slipping down! We spent the night in Jaubari on a farmer's verandah. Food good. Flies bad!

Day 2: On the trail by 6 a.m. Lost the way several times. At a bridge we were quite at a loss where to go next. Waited. Wondered. Then we saw a little old unkempt lady with a big basket of wild pears on her back. She told us the way—"You'll get to some rice fields—they're ours. When you come to an avalanche, go above it." She insisted on giving us some pears. I was dumbfounded by her love and generosity. Then she looked at me and said, "You are Bhagwan" (God). I hastened to tell her that I was an ordinary mortal like she was, but that I served the living God. Tears filled her eyes and she stretched up to touch my face.

The path was hard after that. A lot of climbing. Got bitten or stung by something invisible and we all developed huge itchy welts! Stopped at one p.m., exhausted. Naomi and the men were able to light a fire and make some soup. We ate heartily and set off feeling new. About four-thirty we crossed the rickety suspension bridge at the foot of Barpak hill. The drizzle increased. We were all very glad to stop about six p.m. A couple of little girls carrying vegetables up from the fields led us through the corn fields (corn towering two to four metres high) to their house, a very humble home where we were made welcome. The son, home on leave from the army, was the only one in this large family who could speak Nepali. We had brought rice and lentils along with our main meals and they let us use their firewood to cook it.

Day 3: Arrived in Barpak after a two-hour climb. Received a warm welcome. P.L.'s mother is not a Christian but nevertheless she loves us (and we her!). We saw some sick patients on his verandah and made several house calls. We stopped briefly to speak to a blind man who was grinding corn in a two-stone grinder. Blind since an infant, he seemed to listen eagerly to the gospel. "I believe all that you have said. Please explain it to me." P.L. says he will teach him.

Day 4: Saw about fifty sick in one room of the school. A few were very ill. Pulled some teeth. Made some more house calls. Went for evening meal and worship to a new house where the wife and family of a believer live. Husband is in Hong Kong in the army. The state of the school is pretty pathetic. Hundreds of children are growing up with no schooling. Believers seemed to greatly appreciate our visit. So far no women believers. Hindu headman of the village urged us to come often and to stay longer. They are very anxious that we should have a dispensary there and that we should help in the schools. No government permission.

We took along basic essentials for our meals but we greatly appreciated all the love that went into the preparation. Our menu was spicy potatoes for breakfast, tea and rice and lentils for noon and night.

Day 5: Prayer with the believers. A few last-minute patients. A lady had been carried in the drizzling rain to a two-storey stable near the road. Fond farewells.

The Darondi River is now a raging torrent. At one place, to get around a magnificent waterfall, we had to wade across part of the Darondi to an island and then back again to the bank. We had no trouble on the way up, but in three days the river was fuller. The Lord gave Jim really superhuman strength and wisdom to get us to the other bank, otherwise I would have been swept away. We decided to take a different way which meant crossing the Darondi on a "tween." I ordinarily get a great kick out of crossing rivers, but I was really afraid of this. It was a simple homemade ropeway. The rope was handmade from thin strips of bamboo. Enormous relief to have one's feet on the other side. That was our last main adventure.

Day 6: Arrived home safely. About four p.m. took off those terrible wet soggy boots and rejoiced with our friends over tea and chocolate cake. They had been terribly busy in the dispensary. They too had been through very deep waters. A teenager had died and the family was belligerent and accusing.

Before Helen closed the journal on her monsoon-season journey to Barpak, she penned in the promise of Isaiah 43: "When thou passeth through the waters, I will be with thee; And through the rivers, they shall not overflow thee."

20
The Unfinished Business

Years before, on Palm Sunday, 1954, Helen's spiritual life had taken a great leap forward. Now she felt that there was another step to be taken—some unfinished business.

She had been baptized as an infant in the United Church, a ceremony in which her parents had sincerely dedicated her life to God. She wasn't critical of that tradition, but she grew increasingly convinced that the Scriptures called for baptism to be reserved for believers. One verse spoke loudly and clearly: "Peter replied, 'Repent and be baptized, every one of you, in the name of Jesus Christ for the forgiveness of your sins. And you will receive the gift of the Holy Spirit.'" (Acts 2:38)

The Holy Spirit had already found a prominent place in her life— guiding and directing, giving strength and wisdom. She longed for more of the gifts and fruits of the Spirit, not just for herself, but to make her a more effective servant of Christ.

She longed to be re-baptized as a believer but for various reasons her plans had fallen through. And now it was April, 1968, and the business was still unfinished. She determined to seize the opportunity to talk about baptism with the Anglican bishop Stephen Neil who, at seventy, included a quick visit to Amp Pipal on a tour of overseas missions. Helen had first met Bishop Neil on the campus of the University of Alberta in 1950.

On the evening of his visit to Amp Pipal, the bishop met with the assembled missionaries, and Helen hoped to take him aside later to discuss her baptism before he left for Pokhara the next day. But in the middle of the meeting the medical team was called to an emergency. Four sweating and panting men had arrived at the dispensary with a seventeen-year-old boy named Iman. They laid him on the verandah and waited for Dr. Helen.

Helen stooped down to the boy and unpeeled layers of dirty cloth and banana leaves. She was shocked at the sight. His abdomen had burst open and much of the bowel was lying free on the outside. About thirty-six hours earlier he had fallen down a steep hill and impaled his abdomen on a sharp branch.

"Why did you wait so long to bring him here?" she asked the men.

One man answered, "We came as quickly as we could. For a whole day he lay on the ground calling for help before anyone heard him. He was carried back to our village, but we had to keep him there all night because there was a bad storm. We left as soon as the roosters crowed."

The wiry porters had carried Iman to Amp Pipal in eleven hours, a trip that normally takes a day and a half of hard hiking.

The boy was barely holding on to life. Resuscitation with fluids helped him a little, but there was really no alternative to emergency surgery.

During the operation Helen removed almost two metres of gangrenous bowel and put clamps on the protruding ends. He needed more surgery that could not be done in the simply equipped dispensary. But could he possibly stand the trip to Pokhara?

At 3:30 a.m. Helen was still awake, unable to get Iman off her mind. She called Nora and Beth, who had been up all night with Iman, and they gathered to pray beside his bed. Their prayer was practical and specific. "Lord, we can't do much more for this boy. We need your help. We ask that you touch him and restore his blood pressure to something near normal. If that happens, and if his family agrees, we'll take both as signs to take him to Pokhara."

An hour later they took his blood pressure. It was still below normal, but at least it was measurable. The family gave approval. They decided to go ahead. The exhausted porters were wakened, the nurses prepared food for the trip, and at 6:30 a.m., with not a moment to lose, Helen led the little party toward the Palangtar airfield. One of the porters ran ahead to hold the plane, and even though it was filled with passengers, the pilot, Captain King, an old friend of Helen's, made room for her and cleared an area so the patient could be laid on the floor beside her. She could keep a watchful eye on his stomach tube and intravenous bottle.

The plane arrived in Pokhara, transportation was immediately arranged—a miracle in itself in a town which had only a few cars—and Helen and her patient made the eight-kilometre journey over bumpy roads to the Shining Hospital. An operation had just been cancelled; Iman could be taken to the operating room right away.

He tolerated the procedures better than anyone had expected, but his condition remained precarious.

The following day he seemed a little better. Helen felt content to leave him in the care of the Shining Hospital surgeon.

Helen returned to the airport to book a seat to Palangtar, but the flight was full. She would have to stay in Pokhara for a few days. Was this the opportunity to take care of "the unfinished business"?

A Shining Hospital doctor, Graham Scott-Brown, offered to baptize her in the river but suggested she talk it over with Bishop Neil first. He had flown from Palangtar to Pokhara on the same flight as Helen and Iman.

Early Sunday morning, before he had a chance "to fully put his surplice on," Helen knocked at Bishop Neil's door. She relayed her plans and the bishop gave his approval of a lay Christian performing her baptism.

The stage was set. At 3:00 p.m. on a beautiful Palm Sunday, April 7, 1968, ten persons gathered down by the Seti River for this important event that had been her heart's desire for over ten years.

During the short service, Graham told how Jesus was baptized by John the Baptist and how the Holy Spirit came upon him. This was Helen's wish—to be filled with the Spirit. She walked into the river where Graham immersed her momentarily beneath the surface of the quiet waters. While she stood there dripping wet, he placed his hand on her head and prayed that she might receive the gifts of wisdom and faith.

A deep joy, peace and thanksgiving enfolded her as she climbed the bank out of the river. She rejoined her friends who celebrated with her, singing song after song. She longed for the "gifts of the Spirit" but was admonished by Graham to be patient—"sometimes it is harder for those who are educated to receive the gifts God wants to give."

She remained in Pokhara for one more day before flying back to Palangtar. It was hard to leave Iman and even harder to wait for more than a month before finding out what had happened to him.

Finally, on May 10, Captain King flew his DC-3 at treetop level over the Amp Pipal ridge and tipped his wings—the signal that he had brought Iman back from Pokhara. That tip of the wings set off cheering and rejoicing such as the dispensary had rarely heard before.

The next day Helen examined Iman in the dispensary and declared him "thin as a rake, but alive and functioning well."

She wrote about the young man in her journal, "He has a wonderful smile. He's just a country kid—the type you like to hug! He was in church today."

Iman and his doctor after the successful treatment.

21

A Canadian Farmer
Plants a Dream

Originally intended to be only a small medical work in a small village on a small mountain, the modest dispensary offered the only reliable medical service for half a million people inside a vast circumference.

The Gorkha Project educational work had also progressed far beyond original plans. Amp Pipal had been the first school in the Gorkha District, but others had sprung up to meet the villagers' hunger for education. During the sixties the educational work flourished. In 1961 the mission opened a school at Luitel, about two hours' walk from Amp Pipal, and others followed. Each school began with primary students and gradually added higher grades. These Gorkha schools developed a reputation for graduating students whose academic accomplishments were among the best in the country.

In 1957 the literacy rate in the Gorkha region had been two percent of the population. By the mid-sixties, 2,500 students were enrolled in Gorkha schools started by the UMN.

Jonathan Lindell understood the close connection between eight years of steady medical service and health education in the schools. He stated in a mission report, "Now we see hundreds of students, from thirty surrounding villages, coming to school daily. They are washed and brushed and clean, and have learned modern rules of health."

There were noticeable ripples of change. In 1960 every student but one had scabies and intestinal worms. Five years later, the school population was almost completely free of these hazards to health.

The dispensary played a key role in giving the people hope for relief from rampant disease and malnutrition. The consistent medical help and health teaching, Lindell said, "had gradually turned the thinking of the public. They instinctively go to the dispensary for help, instead of exorcising spirits, paying priests and sacrificing animals."

Trust and confidence in the dispensary health-care team had grown phenomenally. But that could mean only one thing—more patients. The staff knew only too well that the hilly backwoods was still a massive reservoir of illness and disease, and since the doctor's arrival, more seriously ill patients were being brought to the dispensary, which now had a reputation for being able to handle any emergency.

The medical team showed signs of weakening and bending under the unrelenting workload. Helen and the nurses were going flat out from dawn to dusk and were on call at night, looking after the needs of twenty thousand patients a year. In 1964 Nora appealed to UMN headquarters: "We really do need your prayers for health out here. We've never had it like this before with so many [dispensary workers] sick or exhausted."

It was impossible to handle all the patients. Sick people filled the six beds in the *deras* and overflowed into a small annex and even into the hayloft of a nearby stable. The not-so-ill were harboured in a couple of nearby teashops. In the monsoon rain the nurses found it tricky business carrying trays down the slippery slope to patients in the hayloft.

Helen and Jonathan Lindell had talked about the possibility of a small hospital. Was it a goal worth aiming for?

If so, should it be located at Amp Pipal with all the other activities of the Gorkha Project? Or should it be on the flats down by the airstrip? Another possibility was in Bandipur, a large town several hours walk from the airfield in the opposite direction. Where could they be sure to get a good water supply? What location would be most accessible for the thousands of people living in the hills and mountains as far north as the Tibetan border?

It looked like a hospital was needed for this hilly, isolated area of Nepal but, as Helen wrote in a letter, "We had no land, no money and no know-how."

But they saw the need and they had the vision. Most important of all, they had placed their trust and confidence in the Lord who had guided the pioneering party to Amp Pipal in the first place.

They believed that God loved the people of Nepal—as they themselves had grown to love them—and that He would guide and direct them in this matter of a hospital. If it seemed to be His desire that they proceed, He would supply all the resources they needed, as He had done so many times before.

*****

One Sunday evening a retired farmer in Alberta had just tuned in to hear a radio broadcast by Rev. Russell Ross of First United Church, Vancouver. An old friend of Will Huston, Mr. Ross had learned from him about Helen and the Gorkha Project.

"Friends," he said, "I have told you a little of the fine pioneering missionary outreach work to serve the neglected people in the hills of Nepal. These are the people whom Jesus would call 'the least of these my brethren.'

"A hospital is desperately needed. I believe we have a unique opportunity at this time to donate money so that the mission can go ahead and build it. And I think we Western Canadians have a vested interest in this important project; the medical work is under the direction of Dr. Helen Huston from Alberta."

Eleven time zones from Nepal, the Alberta farmer with the responsive heart sat down that same evening, wrote a cheque for one thousand dollars and sent it to the UMN, designating it for Dr. Helen Huston's medical work in the hills.

His letter took a long time to reach Kathmandu, and still longer to be placed in her hand, but Helen was overjoyed at this generous gift.

Immediately she sent him an exuberant thank-you letter, assuring him that the money had come at a most crucial time. After receiving her note, the same man wrote a second cheque, this time for nine thousand dollars, and sent it to be used toward her hospital dream.

Now the notion of a "mountain hospital" no longer lurked quietly in the back of minds at the UMN. This ten thousand dollars provided the impetus they needed. Helen took it as fresh evidence that the time had come to push on with hospital plans.

But even with this money in hand, how practical was it to plan a building project in a remote, almost inaccessible mountainside village? An optimistic hospital building committee, formed in 1964, began to look seriously at the concept. They considered the kind of hospital they would build if—with emphasis on the *if*—a hospital could be built.

Any hospital in Gorkha would have to be kept "simple and homelike" so that villagers and hill people unaccustomed to shiny sterile environments would not be intimidated or made to feel uncomfortable.

The committee debated whether there should be straw mats or beds, eventually deciding that beds would save the backs of nurses and doctors. Space and benches would be provided for *sathis* (friends), because the assistance of friends and relatives was essential when nursing staff were spread so thin.

The government of Nepal gave its approval for a fifteen-bed hospital, and the Mission agreed on the size but insisted upon room for future expansion. They envisioned a large outpatient department and fifteen-bed *dera* accommodation for chronically ill and long-term patients.

But it was choosing the location of the hospital, the most crucial part of the plan, that gave the committee much pause. Land near the airfield at Palangtar was flat and easy to reach from Kathmandu. A road was planned that would pass within three hours' walk. But there was a problem with this choice. At the lower altitude, temperatures were almost unbearable during the hot season.

Even if it meant a long walk from the new road or airfield, it seemed important to keep the medical service as accessible as possible to the roadless hilly areas. The committee agreed to select a site in one of the villages in the hills.

The most important consideration, Helen recalls, was to go where the people wanted them to be. Harmi, a village an hour's walk north from the Amp Pipal ridge, was in some ways a better choice than the site of the mission dispensary. But the local village leaders, mostly Hindus of the Brahmin caste, made it abundantly clear that Christians would not be welcome to work in their village.

Amp Pipal villagers, on the other hand, had welcomed the foreign missionaries to their village from the outset and had grown to appreciate them as reasonable and friendly comrades. They were well aware of the benefits these Christians had brought with them: their children were going to school, farmers were prospering from the practical agricultural training and advice, and their sick and injured were getting the care they needed at the dispensary.

Nor were they blind to the fact that the economy of Amp Pipal had received a great boost since the mission had taken up residence. An entire hospital, with its need for staff and services, would do wonders for the community.

The Amp Pipal site offered some advantages, but the committee foresaw a serious problem: the lack of a reliable source of water, an essential for any hospital. Water for the dispensary had always been carried from a village spring up a steep hill in old kerosene tins. Water surveys had been taken on the slopes of Lig Lig Mountain, and several streams issued from the hillsides during monsoon season, but an ample year-round water supply had not been found.

In February, 1964, Jonathan Lindell flew out from Kathmandu to meet Amp Pipal village leaders to discuss possible hospital locations. The leaders had prepared a strong case.

The mission had "given a good name to Amp Pipal," they said, and it would be a mistake to build a hospital anywhere else.

The determined dozen leaders rested their case in fine style; they presented their good friend, Jonathan, with a healthy young goat.

Jonathan listened with respect to their well-presented arguments, and then, pulling gently on the rope around the goat's neck, he responded in Nepali, "Gentlemen, I appreciate how you feel. But our goal is to choose a site that will serve the people of the whole northern area in the best way possible."

Rubbing the goat's woolly head, he added, "I'm grateful to you for this gift, but I can't accept it if that means we're bound to build the new hospital here." The men nodded their heads and chuckled together. Each side understood the other well.

Jonathan returned to headquarters without making a final decision, leaving the goat behind to provide a feast for workmen constructing a small building in Amp Pipal.

The animal had nothing to do with the eventual choice of a site, but from all angles it did appear that Amp Pipal was the best location. It was close to crossroads, including a major north-south footpath, and was accessible to people living in the folds of hills and valleys extending as far north as the Tibetan border. And it did make sense to locate the hospital close to existing mission projects.

As for the crucial water supply, the mission decided to consult an expert and had a geologist flown in from Kathmandu. After examining seven springs, he recommended tunnelling at one site where he was confident of a good flow of water.

It wasn't that spring after all, but one lower down, that ultimately proved to be the mission's best water source. It flowed just above the *chautara* or resting-place site, at the base of a huge, spreading pipal tree, a twenty-minute downhill walk from the dispensary. Workers found a few good springs, measured the flow, and dug out and cemented a reservoir.

The village scribe signing the land deed.

113

Sloping gently down from the *chautara* were four terraced rice fields owned by a villager. The *Kanchha Mukhia* (village headman) investigated and discovered that this piece of land was for sale. The *panchayat* (village government) was willing to buy it and turn it over free of charge to the mission.

It seemed like a happy arrangement, but the *panchayat* didn't have the cash in hand at the moment. So the mission loaned the *panchayat* the sum of 3707.50 rupees (about $370 Canadian), and by the summer of 1965 the location of Amp Pipal hospital had been legally settled.

Although aesthetics hadn't figured as a high priority in the choice, the *chautara* site was a place of great scenic beauty. The beauty was a bonus.

22

The Gift of an Architect

So now they were bona fide owners of a piece of sloping land by a magnificent spreading pipal tree. And they had some money to get started on construction. But was it still too tall an order to begin a major construction project in this remote area?

It looked as though nothing less than a miracle could do the job. Helen and Jonathan both had ideas about the kind of building that was needed, but their minds could not yet conceive a way to get it built. They both knew that, to be affordable, the building would have to be constructed of locally available materials.

In Kathmandu most buildings were made of sun-dried bricks, but clay in the Gorkha District had never been tried and tested as bricking material for a large building. Houses and sheds could be built with local stone and mud; a much larger hospital building was another matter.

They grappled with details. Forests were disappearing on the hill-sides all over the country to supply wood for cooking fires. Would they be able get a permit to cut trees for lumber? A further problem arose: where could they find workmen with the necessary building skills?

If thatch was not used for the roof, any imported roofing material would need to be flown out from Kathmandu to Palangtar and carried up the side of Lig Lig Mountain. In fact, everything that was not locally made would have to be lugged up the hill for at least four hours on a human beast of burden. The challenge was an awesome one.

The financial challenge was no less daunting. The mission had $10,000 for sure—in fact there were a number of small amounts to be added to this figure—but how bold and forthright can you be in planning a hospital with only that amount of money?

The building committee rested some of its hope for more funds on a visit from a member of the United Church's Board of World Mission. The Reverend Floyd Honey spent a week in Nepal and included a hike to Amp Pipal. He discussed the hospital plans with Helen and Jonathan and supported them all the way, but he could promise no financial help for the Amp Pipal project. The United Church would be hard pressed, he told them, just to make its regular capital grant to the UMN.

The prayers for a miracle grew more determined. One answered prayer came in the form of a young, down-to-earth Australian architect. In April, 1965, Vanne Trompf and his wife had stopped over in Nepal for a "quick visit" on their way to Europe. They had been advised to see a bit of Nepal by friends who knew Howard and Betty Barclay.

Just what happened when they reached Nepal is not all that clear, but the Trompfs' proposed one-week stay extended into two months, and then into six. Vanne was no ordinary architect; he had completed his thesis on the challenges of building in subtropical countries and had already gained experience in India. He wasn't shy about pitching in with the workers, and soon after his arrival in Nepal, he helped to build the mud and stone house of teachers Thomas and Mary Varghese in the village of Luitel.

The UMN hired Vanne for six months, first to draw up plans for a girls' high school in Kathmandu and, when he finished that project, to design the Gorkha Hospital in Amp Pipal. On his first visit to the *chautara* site, he took copious notes and measurements, and then, over hot glasses of Nepali tea, spent long periods talking with Helen and the nurses about the optimal size of the wards, lighting required in the operating room, facilities needed in the out-patient department and so on. There was no master plan to go by, but Helen drew heavily on her recollection of the layout of Shanta Bhawan and Tansen hospitals and Vanne adapted the concepts to the Amp Pipal setting.

Within a few days, the innovative and imaginative Australian had mapped out in his head a rough idea of the hospital layout. And by the end of six months, he had completed a pile of detailed drawings, ready to be placed in the hands of a builder. His plans called for a complex of hospital buildings to be tucked in snugly and neatly on the sloping site and to reflect the openness and simplicity of Nepali building style. All of his work he offered to the mission free of charge. (Small wonder that Helen took to calling him "God's gift to us out here.")

At 3:15 on the afternoon of October 5, 1965, a gathering of fifty to sixty people assembled on the *maidan* (flat, grassy area) just above the big pipal tree. It was the historic day for the formal land transfer for the Amp Pipal hospital, the largest construction project ever to be undertaken in these remote hills.

The ceremony began when Shambu Lal, a short Nepali man with thinning hair, head of the village governing body, stood up and without fanfare, began to address the crowd. In his almost inaudible

Shambu Lal addressing the crowd at the land transfer ceremony.

voice he concluded his prepared speech: "Our United Mission friends, you have been working among us for more than seven years. We are glad to know that you plan to build a hospital for our sick people. Now I would like to ask my father, the *Mukhia*, to come forward to present the land document for the hospital."

Actually, the *Mukhia* had already come forward and was standing beside Shambu Lal, beaming with pride that his son could make such an important speech. Clad in a white *doti* that left his legs bare from mid-thigh down, the bandy-legged elderly gentleman, village headman of bygone years, stepped forward. With dignity befitting the duty he was about to perform, he accepted from his son the deed for the land.

Then a tall, dark-haired woman, striking in appearance in a cream-coloured sari, rose from her place on the grassy slope. Over her sari she wore a bright green flowered shawl, and her long hair had been braided and pinned up for the important event.

The occasion was more special than ever for Helen, because both her mother and her sister were present. Edith, who was then a spunky 72-year-old, had been carried up in a "dandy," a boat-shaped wooden chair supported by poles on the shoulders of three men. Mary had walked the full distance, with a helping hand over the rough and steep parts from Futtay Bahadur, Helen's porter.

Helen listened intently to Shambu Lal's speech, powerless to hide the sparkle in her eye and the faint smile that curled her lips. As she reached out her hands to accept the land document the *Mukhia* presented to her with both hands extended, her whole face blossomed with joy.

"*Dhanyabad, Hajur* (Thank you, respected sir)," said Helen, accepting the document as superintendent of medical work for the Gorkha Project. She looked straight into the eyes of the old man and then down to the simple, hand-inscribed sheets that felt like a gift from heaven.

Jonathan Lindell, now Executive-Secretary of the UMN, gave a short speech. Project director Howard Barclay then addressed the hillside gathering, thanking the local *panchayat* for their cooperation in donating the land. In a closing prayer in Nepali, he gave thanks for that day and dedicated to God the sloping plot of land, and the building to be erected on that site.

Then it was all over. And like all ceremonies in Nepal, it had to be followed by tea—hot, sweet, spicy tea served in glasses and accompanied by salty biscuits. Cheeky brown and white mynah birds,

swooping down as close to the gathering as they dared, snapped up eatables that fell to the ground.

People mingled and chatted, but everyone's attention was focussed primarily on the easel Vanne had set up to display the sketched floor plans of the future hospital. Curious villagers clustered around the easel asking, "When will the hospital be built? Will I be able to get good stomach medicine? Will the doctor be able to do operations there?"

Vanne Trompf describes the hospital plans.

Although Edith and Mary understood not a word of the proceedings, they could still celebrate, knowing that this was a giant step toward "the hospital in the hills" of their daughter and sister.

The prospects of the hospital going from plans on paper to a real building looked promising; by now there were just enough funds on hand to begin construction, and workers could make a start on cutting trees anytime. The committee trusted that an experienced builder could be found to implement the plans of Vanne Trompf.

Only one problem made Helen feel uneasy after the ceremony was over. In a few days she would be walking out of Amp Pipal to begin a year's furlough, and the mission had been unable to find anyone to replace her. For an entire year, there would be no doctor at Amp Pipal—again.

23

Not Your Average Passenger

"I'm sorry, but I'm afraid you can't take that microscope. It won't fit under the seat."

"Ma'am, the height, width and depth of your two pieces of luggage must not exceed 270 centimetres. They're close, you say? Well, no, they're actually 330 centimetres. I'm sorry. There's no way we can call that bag a purse."

Helen Huston is not your average airline passenger. Pity the poor harmless clerk at the check-in counter who has no inkling that this friendly-looking woman with the gentle approach has a will as unbending as iron.

On one journey, she innocently deposited her baggage on the weigh scales at the airport in Bangkok, Thailand. She usually had loads of paraphernalia on her way back to Nepal from Canada and this time was no exception. The bags, boxes and odd-shaped parcels weighed in at 55 kilograms, slightly in excess of the permitted limit of 20 kilograms. The discrepancy didn't seem to register with the bleary-eyed clerk who absent-mindedly wrote "2 x 10 kg." on her ticket.

"They actually weigh a little more than that," Helen protested mildly. The clerk heard her well enough but proceeded to tag all the various pieces of baggage and pass them through the system without a word.

It wasn't the first time that the airlines had bent the rules for Dr. Helen Huston. She travelled with microscopes, wheelchair parts, sometimes entire wheelchairs, inflatable cushions, catheters, sutures and other sundry medical supplies, as well as gifts from and for various people.

On one of her excursions, the desk clerk at the Western Airlines counter looked at the mountain of gear and then at a huge green shoulder bag she carried, and said, "I'll get the supervisor."

Called to give direction on the baggage problem, the supervisor figured that, by calling the green bag a handbag, they could treat it as carry-on luggage. So far, so good. She had made it past the counter but still had the security check ahead of her. Security officers became very suspicious when the contents of the fat green bag showed up as odd metal shapes. Soon, piece by piece, every item of medical equipment was lined up on the counter leaving only the forlorn, collapsed green bag.

Helen had a good share of strong points, but getting organized for a trip was not one of them. She states the obvious when she says, "I'm not usually ready early for a trip," and anyone who has ever witnessed her last-minute packing has stood amazed at the chaos that accompanied the rush.

Said her sister Mary, "There is always an element of excitement and surprise, as well as disbelief of success, seeing Helen off so laden down with bags and boxes."

And a friend, who has more than once helped her pack and seen her off from Canada, described the experience as hilarious. Mildred Sullivan recalls the monumental effort in the summer of 1982 as several people squeezed and compressed against the laws of nature to close one of Helen's stuffed, overflowing suitcases.

Mildred then drove her to the Seattle airport to catch the flight for her return trip to Nepal. As usual, there was a problem with the luggage at the counter. She had one suitcase too many. An excess

121

baggage charge would have to be paid for it on several airlines, all the way to Kathmandu. This just wouldn't do; there must be some solution.

It took only minutes for Mildred and Helen to rope two of the bags together, and they returned to the weigh-in counter with a monstrous piece of luggage that could hardly be lifted. It seemed to satisfy the clerk who just stood there, eyes rolled heavenward. Somehow or other they all parted friends.

24

Stone Blocks and Mud Mortar

Rounding the north side of Lig Lig Mountain, Helen finally caught a glimpse of the *chautara* site. It was December, 1966, and she had just arrived back from furlough in Canada, wondering how plans were progressing for the Amp Pipal hospital.

She wasn't disappointed that walls weren't already standing. In fact, the foundation wasn't even laid. But they had staked out the site and, wonder of wonders, had found a builder!

A few months earlier, the UMN had succeeded in obtaining an experienced American building contractor. Supported by the Mennonite Board of Missions, Jim Miller and his wife Pauline signed on for a three-year term. They had already completed their orientation and language study, and Jim had studied the plans and drawings that called for construction on two levels, fit into the natural contours of the land. The overall floor area was estimated at 1,078 square metres, unbelievable luxury after the four and one-half by nine-metre two-storey dispensary.

Jim rolled up his sleeves and began the construction project in January, a month after Helen's return. He hired 150 Nepali workmen and, from the first day, consulted with them as equals and often sought their advice. Doing the work of bulldozers, men with picks and shovels waded into the painstaking job of excavating the site. Others hauled in large quantities of lumber, mostly sal wood, that had been felled and trimmed entirely by hand.

The hospital under construction.

The local workmen had no experience in making or laying bricks, but they did know how to work skillfully with stone. Jim decided to construct all major walls with shaped stones, using mud as mortar. Workmen relied on an iron crowbar to dislodge stones from a nearby hill; men and women carried them to the building site in *dokos*.

Some materials were carried up from the Palangtar airfield, including bags of cement powder for pouring the floor and sheets of corrugated aluminum for the roof. Almost thirty-five thousand kilograms (about seventy-six thousand pounds) of building material was

124

flown from Kathmandu to Palangtar and hauled into Amp Pipal on the backs of porters.

After less than a year of digging, sawing and stone-cutting, the walls of the ward for female patients were almost complete, and Jim had made a start on the first staff residence. Quiet Amp Pipal had been transformed into a virtual hive of valiant community effort. The old *chautara* site simply buzzed with activity.

*****

On the opposite side of the world, efforts were less physically demanding but equally valiant as individuals were gathering the funds needed to complete and equip the Amp Pipal hospital.

No one had any idea how much money would be enough. The UMN had approved a capital budget of 200,000 rupees ($20,000 U.S.) to begin the first phase. The government of Nepal had approved the hospital's construction, but on the condition that it be built without any government funding.

Jonathan wrote to ask for assistance from Oxfam, admitting candidly, "In an interior, isolated place in the mountains of Nepal, where no such building work has ever been undertaken, it is impossible for us to estimate what this program will cost."

As the walls went up, the money came in from many sources: $20,000 from the American Presbyterians; $10,000 from the United Church of Canada; $3,500 from Oxfam.

The retired farmer from Alberta had started it, and soon he was joined by men and women, children and senior citizens from Victoria, British Columbia to St. Johns, Newfoundland. Some gave pennies, a few gave a thousand dollars or more—but all gifts were precious. One couple in Nova Scotia sent their first gift in 1968; to this day they continue to send monthly contributions.

Many of the United Church contributers had read the article "Helen Huston's Mission in the Clouds" in the *Observer*. But a great deal of support came from elsewhere.

In Calgary's Hillhurst United Church the need of the new hospital for an X-ray machine caught the fancy of the ninety boys and girls in the Sunday School Primary Department. Their teacher explained that an X-ray can actually take pictures of your insides, to see if you have pneumonia or a broken arm.

The kids huddled together: what if you had a tummy ache? Would an X-ray really help then?

They took a big cardboard box, cut a slot in the top for coins, and on one side drew a picture of a little boy bent over and grimacing with a tummy ache. Underneath it said: "An X-ray found out what was wrong with him; just see the other side of the box."

On the other side they had made a large drawing of the same boy standing in front of an X-ray machine. In his tummy you could see a plateful of chips, a box of smarties and a huge banana split with a red cherry on top!

Within two weeks the children had raised $200 on their own, and soon the rest of the congregation had joined in.

More funds came from people who had heard of the Amp Pipal hospital during Helen's recent furlough in Canada. While in Camrose, Alberta, Helen had spent an evening with her friend, Dorothy Gibson, and her Explorer Girls Club. After the evening's program ended, many of the girls held back, wanting to know how they could help Helen and the hospital.

When Dorothy suggested the girls organize a bottle drive, Helen spoke up. "Let me tell you," she said, "what could be done in Nepal with the deposit money from four beer bottles. Forty cents will pay for three days' medicine for someone with tuberculosis. It will buy porridge for a malnourished child for ten days, and it will cover a patient's basic hospital costs for two days."

"Will forty cents buy anything for the new hospital?" Dorothy asked, and Helen answered, "It will pay a day's wages for a man carrying stone to build the walls."

At the end of a week's hunting by the enthusiastic Explorer Girls a mountain of cans and bottles was deposited at the bottle depot. A young Asian girl, a recent arrival in Canada from Vietnam, was judged the most successful collector and was crowned by her Explorer friends as "Queen of the Cans."

At least part of the new Amp Pipal hospital was built by old redeemed cans and bottles from the ditches and back lanes of Camrose, Alberta!

Every contribution, large or small, supported the hospital's agenda to serve the needy people of the Gorkha District. In the end, CIDA (Canadian International Development Agency) matched the amounts raised privately. The final tally for construction and equipping of the hospital was 878,800 rupees. At ten rupees per U.S. dollar, it was a miraculous achievement.

Except for the days of the drenching monsoon season, not an hour of daylight was wasted throughout 1968. The in-patient section was finished, the out-patient department and the operating room were nearing completion, and a start was made on a second house for staff. The hospital was fully wired, thanks to trainee-electricians from the UMN's technical institute in the town of Butwal.

Jim Miller knew that Helen and her co-workers were carrying a maximum stress load and he was anxious to see it lightened. In their old clothes-closet dispensary, they saw a record 25,308 patients in 1968 and performed 288 operations. Even if only one quarter of the hospital was roofed and usable, it would make their job so much easier. But Jim advised them to hold on for just a few more months at the dispensary; if doctors and nurses stayed out of the way, carpenters and finishers could work more quickly. They agreed to keep going for a while longer.

On March 25, 1969, they made their historic move to the new hospital, still far from complete (in fact, half the hospital was still open to the skies) but more or less usable.

From the dispensary all medicines, supplies and instruments, records and documents were carried the twenty-minute walk down the hill in *dokos*. Everyone helped, including patients and their relatives as well as staff and students from the school. The evacuation worked so smoothly that the medical team missed only two days in seeing new patients.

The triumphant communal procession to the stone and mud hospital lasted all day, and by nightfall the eleven-year dispensary era was over.

In early April, 1969, Helen wrote, "Today is Good Friday and the hospital is open! . . . The O.R. has no roof, but the roofing is on the way, carried up on heads of men, women and boys! Wonderful if it can be put on before the rains. The old *deras* are now empty; we've brought down the TB patients. We've only the seven old wooden beds brought down from the deras, but we have an in-patient count of 23, mostly on mats on the floor."

Helen expected more beds to arrive any day. Months before, she had noticed an ad in a brochure listing surplus Canadian government materials. Sixteen lightweight, collapsible metal beds were for sale for the bargain price of $605, shipping and delivery costs included! She ordered them for the new hospital and was thrilled when they survived the long journey from Canada and the haul up the hills into Amp Pipal.

The sixteen bed frames were sturdy, all right, but they had one major fault. They were just too high for Nepali patients to climb into. A hacksaw amputation of five centimetres off each metal leg corrected the problem. Only too happy to get up off their *gundris* (rice mats) the Nepali patients seemed to rest quite comfortably on beds that had previously held holdup men and embezzlers from St. Vincent de Paul Penitentiary in Quebec.

Nothing at the new Amp Pipal hospital was "average." An uneven collection of stone-walled structures, it didn't look like a hospital, and in fact, in the annals of the world's hospital buildings, it probably stood alone. The metal penitentiary beds were a perfect match for the overall decor, which bore more resemblance to a prison than a health facility.

Her dispensary experience had convinced Helen that the hospital had to be kept simple, perhaps leaning a bit toward the primitive, and reasonably clean, but not too clean. She made concessions to culture, but drew the line at hawking and spitting on the floor. In Nepal, spitting is not considered uncouth or ill-mannered. In most villages, the day is ushered in with the sounds of adults and children raucously clearing their throats and nasal passages.

The toughest challenge Helen faced was to find and hire more staff. The small team of "kindred spirits" from the dispensary would not be enough to handle the expanded workload. Nearly every evening, she laboured beside her kerosene lamp, drawing up lists of needed hospital staff, ordering equipment and supplies and working on plans and budgets.

She had only two experienced Western missionary nurses (including Val Collett, who had just recovered from tuberculosis), Naomi, a dependable nurse-aide, and Jagat, who had become an indispensable member of the staff. She could hire local cleaners, night watchmen and orderlies, but where on earth could she find more nurse-aides? She decided that her only hope was to train local girls.

Sita was one of the village girls chosen for training. A bright and alert sixteen-year-old, she had gone as far as class three at school but lived in a society that saw little reason to educate girls. She hadn't even been taught to count to a hundred in her language.

Sita began her hospital training as an apprentice and, at the same time, was tutored in her general education by Annama, a South Indian teacher–social worker who had joined the Gorkha Project. She progressed to the position of doctor's assistant in out-patients and, when she worked on wards, was able to read doctors' orders, written in English.

Helen trusted Sita's judgment; if Sita called her for an emergency in the middle of the night, she didn't hesitate, but would grab a flashlight and be off to the hospital.

Those were the times when she longed for a second doctor, someone to share the twenty-four-hour-a-day, seven-day-a-week responsibility. Wouldn't it be wonderful, she thought as she looked up at the black, star-studded sky, if that doctor could be a surgeon—to cope with the multitude of injuries, fractures, abdominal conditions and complications of childbirth.

25

The Living Word

On the hillside overlooking the hospital site, Helen and a Finnish friend soaked in the sun's warmth and light and watched the activity below. It was a few months before the official March, 1969, opening.

Helen began to sing, and Lainna joined in on her spontaneous expression of worship. Then Lainna shared what was on her mind. She told Helen, "God desires that this should not be an ordinary hospital. He wants everyone who comes to it to have the opportunity to hear the Good News. The workmen finishing the construction, the patients and relatives and the staff. And Helen, He wants you to be responsible for seeing that it does become the hospital of the Living Word."

It was their custom to sing and pray together; this time they prayed for the scene at their feet and for the role of the hospital in years to come.

Helen desired nothing more than to tell others about the love of Jesus. But how would everyone have the chance to hear? In the dispensary on most days, so many sick people needed attention that she had no time to speak to them about the really important matters in life.

The government was making things difficult. In fact, the mission had to sign an agreement which prohibited preaching or proselytizing. Open evangelism was clearly impossible but many people asked questions and some hungered to know more about the God of the missionaries and Nepali Christians.

The vision seemed clear enough; it should be a hospital of the Living Word and the Lord had commissioned Helen to make it so. Like Moses, she felt unequal to the task. But if He had called her, she would do her best to obey.

His first instruction was to talk about Jesus with the first patient she saw at the next out-patient clinic.

The assignment didn't seem overly difficult until she met her first patients. They were a husband and wife. The husband had brought his wife to ask about a patch of fungus on her leg. This wasn't even a serious disease that might have opened an opportunity for prayer and counselling.

Helen looked after the fungus problem, wondering how this Hindu couple would respond to a word about Jesus. As they were about to leave the room, she casually mentioned, "We're going to be celebrating Christmas soon."

The husband answered, "Yes, you worship Jesus and we worship Krishna." She was in the midst of considering an answer to his statement when he added, "I've read seventeen chapters of the Bible, but now, since I've moved, I have nobody to teach me."

She gave this couple some Christian booklets before going off for a meeting with the staff. "I met that man again on one of my rare visits to Kathmandu," she recalls. "We sat together on the plane and he asked if I remembered him. I don't usually have an easy time remembering faces, but I did remember him and asked about his wife's leg. He told me he had just had surgery for cancer and a young Nepali man had visited him at the hospital and taught him from the Bible every evening."

This was the first fruit of the Hospital of the Living Word, although

Helen candidly admits that she, and the other Christians on staff, didn't do as much as they could have. "We were always so pressed for time," she explains. "There were so many government rules to follow and we couldn't hold evangelistic meetings. What we longed and hoped for was that each one of the Christian staff would be right with Jesus and each other, and that would open up ways to share."

Hers was the duty to sow the seed; whether it grew or not she left in God's hands.

26
Tested—And Not
Found Wanting

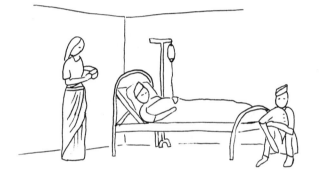

During that first year in the half-finished hospital building, Dr. Helen and her nurses started to collect a waiting list of patients needing elective surgery. Shanta Bhawan's medical director, Dr. Gordon Mack, had already offered to hike up the hills for two days of surgery, and the dates were set for the coming October.

The monsoon skies cleared and the clear fresh days of October arrived, but there was still no operating room at Amp Pipal. No one wanted to postpone the surgery, so two frantic days were invested in transforming a small storage room, slated to be the female ward upon completion of the building, into an improvised O.R.

Working with nurse Beth Brunnemaier and builder Stan Kamp (who succeeded Jim Miller) Helen struggled to get things ready for the surgical team, due to arrive on Sunday afternoon. The hospital's three-kilowatt generator was called into service to provide power for a couple of sixty-watt light bulbs, and a motorcycle headlight, powered by a twelve-volt battery, was on stand-by as a backup.

By mid-evening, Helen and her helpers were feeling quite proud of their little O.R. and its ingenious equipping, when all plans to complete the job had to be put aside.

Two porters carrying a woman in a *doli* arrived at Amp Pipal and burst on the quiet hospital scene. Gasping for breath, they told Helen that the woman had been in labour for three days, and a day ago the pains had suddenly become severe with no let-up and no progress.

Helen pushed aside the first thought that came to her mind: if only this emergency could have come a day later, the surgical team would have been there to handle it. But there was no waiting for tomorrow. The makeshift operating room would be in use tonight.

She started intravenous fluids to prepare the woman for surgery and then went home to gain strength for her own body and soul. She ate supper, read up on the surgical procedure and spent a few minutes in prayer.

Under the homemade spotlight she performed the operation, finding, as she had fully expected, a large tear in the uterus and the baby dead. She closed the ruptured area as best she could.

The young woman withstood the operation and did well afterwards. The very first operation in the half-finished, make-do hospital had literally saved someone's life.

It was a gratifying experience for the whole team. But if Helen had any feelings of pride or satisfaction in accomplishment, they were well hidden. As a servant of the Lord, she was simply enabled to do what was necessary.

Dr. Mack and the anesthetist, Dr. Nelson Nix, arrived on schedule and set to work from dawn until 10 p.m. for the next two days. Their long list of operations included two harelip repairs in children, cleaning out an infected shinbone, and plastic surgery on a teenage boy whose face had been badly burned as a child.

For Helen it was pure joy to work beside "the tremendous indefatigable surgical team." She had comments too for her own hospital staff: "They were terrific. They not only threw themselves into the double work and hours—they loved it!"

The little hospital in the hills had passed its first major test.

27

Cholera Epidemic

It was the holiday part of her 1970–71 furlough, and Helen had decided to relax thoroughly and enjoy her family and friends in the lazy days of a Camrose, Alberta summer. Here was a world far removed from the stresses and strains of Third World living. On top of the easy living, she was really enjoying all the conveniences of home, especially the clean and modern bathrooms!

But she could not stop the Third World from coming into her living room—via modern communication. Along with television viewers around the world, she watched with mounting horror the catastrophic conflict between East and West Pakistan and the tragic forced evacuation of thousands of families from their homes.

It all began when East Pakistan (now Bangladesh), simmering from unfair treatment by the wealthier West, sought independent nationhood. In March, 1971 when the President of West Pakistan sent in

Helen relaxing with her parents in Camrose, Alberta.

troops to quell the uprising and to "re-occupy" the rebellious East, warfare broke out.

From the insulated comfort in her peaceful native country, Helen watched scenes of streams of refugees crossing the border from East Pakistan. Almost ten million—in a single day as many as forty thousand joined the procession to seek protection in West Bengal, a province of India already grossly overpopulated.

She read in Canadian newspapers that resource-stretched India had launched a campaign to feed the massive influx. Housing during the monsoon rains presented an enormous challenge. Violence threatened to spill across the border to India, which resented the persecution of Hindus by the Muslim majority. The Indian government designated the border a restricted area and deployed large concentrations of troops at border points.

Finally Helen heard an appeal from World Vision for volunteers to help at the refugee camps. She immediately requested and was granted approval to spend her remaining furlough time in West Bengal. She phoned the World Vision office in Canada and boarded a jet for India.

The World Vision representative who met her in Calcutta did not even try to hide his doubts about her ability to handle the frightful conditions in a refugee camp. But she assured him that massive tragedy was something she had seen before, starting with the Kumbh Mela disaster seventeen years earlier.

But the doubts and warnings were justified. She was not prepared for the spectacle that confronted her on the day they manoeuvred their jeep over dirt roads north of Calcutta to within a few kilometres of the border. Sounds of gunfire and shelling filled the air. Jammed into a series of low-lying, thatch-roofed huts and three canvas tents were twenty thousand people. Blankets and quilts were spread on the roofs in a futile attempt to keep out the monsoon rains. Ill-clad children huddled together, shivering in the rain and mud. Every accessible tree had been felled for fuel, but the wood was too wet to build a fire for cooking. A handful of latrines hadn't been able to cope with the sewage. Flies swarmed everywhere as soon as the rains let up for a moment.

Helen's reaction was normal. "I wanted to get away from the place as quickly as I could, but I hated myself for it. Anything, just to get out, to get home, to get dry, to get into clean clothes."

But there was no going back. There was work to be done. In that sense, Helen was far better off than the refugees, for they had nothing to distract them from their misery.

Many were well-educated people, like the graduate engineer who, driven out by the local Muslims, had lost everything in the flight from his homeland. The few possessions he had carried were taken by soldiers before he reached the border.

Great numbers of people had sought temporary shelter in long concrete culverts which had been stored in piles on top of one another. Two to four feet in diameter, these cramped quarters offered protection from the rain, but like rabbits trapped in a burrow, the tube people were unable to sit or even to lie comfortably. They were the first to fall prey to bronchitis, pneumonia, dysentery and scabies.

On a rare break from her work at the camp, Helen talked with a Mr. Sen, a lawyer from Calcutta who had been organizing clubs that he called "Youth for Bangladesh." He had enlisted the help of young people to build latrines, move the culverts to higher ground, and scrounge for material to build small huts. A former champion swimmer, he cheerfully boosted spirits, encouraging the people to keep hope alive for "the day we'll go back home."

Helen and Mr. Sen found they had many common interests. One of their conversations she still remembers vividly.

"There is no God," he commented, as they walked one day through the congested camp. "How could any God allow human beings to exist in such misery?"

"But I'm sure there is a God, a loving God," replied Helen. "It's man's wickedness and sin that has caused these people to live in such a sorrowful state."

If both the doubter and the believer thought they were seeing the worst of the human condition in this refugee camp, they were wrong. News came that the fearsome water-borne disease, cholera, had hit the neighbouring camp, Laickipur.

Cholera. A disease capable of destroying its victims in less than twenty-four hours from uncontrollable diarrhea and vomiting. A disease so terrifying that many refugees fled in fear when they heard of the outbreak in their camp, only to risk carrying the germs with them and spreading it further. On her arrival at Laickipur, Helen saw distraught and panic-stricken people running away. Others were screaming and pleading for help that was not there.

As soon as she set foot into the camp, a woman gripped her hand and implored her to come with her. Her fifteen-year-old son, in good health the day before, had stopped breathing by the time they reached their hut. The sobbing mother could not be comforted, and Helen, not knowing the Bengali language, could only embrace her and offer a short prayer in English.

It was a grim task, trying to identify those who looked salvageable and decide who should receive the limited amount of intravenous saline solution—the young, the family breadwinner, the mother of children? Even the worst cases had a good hope of being saved if sufficient saline could be given in that first critical twenty-four-hour period.

Working with flashlights and dashing through the rain from one hut to another that first night, Helen and a few helpers often lost their way in the maze of identical shacks. It was impossible to keep track of the patients receiving intravenous fluids, but they did not stop moving forward, even for a moment, until the last bottle of saline was gone.

No ear could escape the heart-wrenching wailing and sobbing that filled the humid night as family after family lost parents or children.

Within a few days, British volunteers and local officials built a "hospital." Between two rows of huts they hoisted a big tarpaulin over vertical bamboo poles and beneath this sheltering roof proceeded to make one-half-metre-wide hospital beds from slats of bamboo. The odorless "rice-water" diarrhea from the two or three patients lying on each bed would trickle down between the slats onto a layer of sawdust or shavings sprinkled with chloride of lime.

No sooner were the beds built than they were filled with gaunt, hollow-eyed, desperately thirsty cholera victims. Under this sheltering roof, Helen could monitor her patients properly, several at a time on every wooden cot. As soon as patients showed signs of recovery, usually by starting to pass urine again, they were sent out to make room for more.

Family members at patient's bedside during cholera epidemic.

Just as the system began to work smoothly, the Indian authorities issued a new order to all foreigners. They were to leave the refugee camps at dusk each day and return to bases away from the "sensitive" border areas.

How could Helen leave two or three dozen patients who were receiving intravenous fluids around the clock? She hit upon a solution, rather unorthodox medically, but otherwise ingenious. She set the intravenous bottles up in tandem, committed the little hospital into God's hands, and left up to twenty patients under the supervision of the Bengali night watchman who was trained only to turn off a finished bottle of solution.

On some mornings Helen would tramp through the mud in her rubber boots to the hospital under the tarpaulin to find that one or two patients had died during the night. But more commonly several had weathered the storm and life was returning to their drawn, pinched faces. No one was talking of victory but in times to come

Helen was able to write that "several hundreds of lives have been saved."

The onslaught finally showed signs of waning in Laickipur, only to break out in Dasbara, another camp a few kilometres away. Here, the medical team faced an ordeal even worse than Laickipur.

At first it seemed it would be easier, because this camp was slightly better prepared for the epidemic. The camp commandant already had a thatched-roof hospital built and several bamboo beds were finished. But when patients began to arrive before the last beds were built, the carpenters fled, leaving their tools behind.

With the help of a couple of Indian Catholic nursing sisters the medical team worked furiously for days on end. On July 16 Helen wrote in a report: *"Yesterday was particularly hard as we were working like mad on those admitted while outside, and often inside, people were coming and imploring us to care for their loved ones whom they had brought and left on the grass outside. Many had lost three or four relatives in the past few days."*

Close to the end of another exhausting day, five and a half weeks after arriving in West Bengal, Helen met defeat. She was informed that she had two hours to get out of the camp and would not be allowed to return. The Indian army had issued the command that all foreigners must be out waiting on the highway by evening, ready to be transported away from the refugees.

That same day, with a hospital already full, ten oxcarts loaded with men, women and children had arrived at the makeshift hospital. Without her, only two minimally trained medical assistants remained to care for these people.

To desert them all now was almost unthinkable. In fact, it pained her more than anything else she had seen or heard in West Bengal. Boarding the army truck that came to take her away, she felt weighted down and numbed by the suddenness of it all.

In a circular letter to friends and supporters, Helen described the cholera epidemic in one brief paragraph that concluded with her own final comment on the incredible experience: "Lord, awaken men's consciences everywhere to care."

28

Soft but No Pushover

Life would never be quite the same again. In the refugee camps she had seen human misery and degradation such as few others had ever witnessed. Searing memories of sunken-eyed cholera victims and wailing relatives would never leave her.

She had seen great suffering in others—and was prepared to face it herself. ". . . as Christians we are to expect suffering. Jesus was tempted like we are and he suffered. We have the privilege of being partakers of his suffering."

These seemed like strange words coming from a fun-loving person like Helen.

Suffering, for her, came in the form of stressful administrative work. The next three years as Medical Superintendent of Amp Pipal Hospital would turn out to be the most difficult years of her life.

"I have no skills in administration," she once said, and then added with feeling, "I mean zero!"

For years before she left Amp Pipal for her 1970 furlough, the demands of leadership weighed heavily upon her. She coped in most areas, failed in a few. Completing the hospital building, staffing and equipping the various departments, teaching and reaching out into the community—all important functions of her job as a medical superintendent—vied for time when every waking moment could have been spent treating fractures and operating and dealing with serious illnesses.

New administrative trails in Amp Pipal needed to be blazed every day. The challenge of making the transition from the dispensary to the new building, from an intimate handful of workers to an institution with a staff of fifty, fell mainly on her shoulders.

Helen, Medical Director of Amp Pipal Hospital, at her desk.

She often walked home for lunch feeling wrung out by the enormous and unrelenting pressure. After years as the only doctor, experiencing great joy and terrible sorrow, she was now at the point of exhaustion.

Happily, friends supplied small encouragements, such as a simply strung multi-party telephone system that allowed her to check on a patient during the night and then catch a few more hours' sleep. When big problems loomed in front of her, it helped to think about the little mercies.

The greatest relief of pressure came from the United States, in the form of a husband and wife surgeon-pediatrician team. Tom and Cynthia Hale, with their two young sons, were already happily adjusted to the Amp Pipal scene when Helen returned from furlough in 1971.

During their decade of association in Amp Pipal, Helen and Tom were of one heart, although not always of one mind. They often held opposing viewpoints on medical or administrative matters. But because both tended to be conciliators, they sometimes surprised each other the morning after a disagreement, finding that they had both "gone over to the other side."

In the early Huston-Hale months, more than a hundred workmen still laboured at the site, building more furniture, completing houses on the hillside for the staff, and carrying in essential supplies such as wheelchairs, stretchers, parts of the operating table and various surgical instruments. Usually discards from other hospitals, the equipment was a virtual treasure to Amp Pipal.

In deference to a culture which considers white the colour of death, beds were covered with coloured sheets and plaid bedspreads. Antiseptics and disinfectant solutions were used rather more sparingly than in "regular" hospitals. The walls, floors and windows were sturdy and constructed to last, but by design they weren't scrubbed to shine and sparkle.

From beginning to end, Helen's push for simplicity and economy ensured that the village people would feel comfortable at the hospital. It also served to keep the costs down, for she was determined that hospital treatment would remain affordable to villagers, most of whom were subsistence farmers surviving on what they could grow on small plots of land. Still, some patients would not even come, and some would choose to go home to die, rather than risk bankruptcy for the family in order to pay for treatment that could not guarantee a cure.

*****

Helen's ability to look for the best in other people tended to bring out the best. But she had blind spots too and tended to overlook their frailties and weaknesses. Carried to the extreme, it created problems.

Helen served as one of the members of the Amp Pipal church committee when evidence was uncovered that a local believer had broken trust in a serious financial matter. When he was faced with questions and flatly denied responsibility, Helen took him at his word. Further investigation proved the charges to be true, but no disciplinary action was taken by the committee because Helen insisted on giving the man another chance.

These second and third chances and merciful judgments sometimes had the happy consequence of turning a person's life around.
But at other times, they adversely affected the smooth running of the
hospital.

A locally trained staffer was placed in charge of the treatment room
where he changed dressings, applied plaster casts and performed
minor surgery. A capable fellow, he unfortunately developed a surly
and pompous attitude toward other staff members. He considered it
a final blow to be made responsible to another employee he considered
inferior.

Using bully tactics, he incited a handful of troublemakers to gain
control over the hospital staff and threatened another staff member
late one night: "Watch out, or you'll spend the rest of your life in a
wheelchair."

The threat was reported to the medical director, but before action
could be taken, Helen rushed to his defence. In a four-page hand-
written report, she described the thoughts and feelings that she felt
must have been running through his mind:

*"I confess that my behaviour has been like an ornery ox which has
resisted discipline. . . . I admit that many others have encouraged me to
be a troublemaker in the hospital. . . . I want to run the best emergency
and out-patient room in Nepal."*

It was an eloquent plea, designed to express all the noble sentiments
hidden in this man's soul—the only problem being, they weren't there.
Confronted with a variety of serious charges against him, he vehe-
mently denied every last charge and railed viciously against his
accusers, with not a single word of regret. The decision then became
an easy one. He was fired from the staff and the hospital immediately
became a more wholesome place to work.

All the ingredients for strength in diversity, but also for conflict and
tension, could be found side by side at the hospital in Amp Pipal. At
that time the United Mission to Nepal consisted of two hundred
missionaries from more than a dozen countries. Teachers from Japan
found themselves on the same team with agriculturists from Finland,
and nurses from the United States or Canada, with engineers from
Australia. The tremendous variety in culture, mannerisms and behaviour was normally no problem for Helen, who could get along easily
with most people.

144

But at least one relationship, with a missionary colleague from the British Isles, almost got the better of her.

She first met Morag Stewart at Shanta Bhawan Hospital in 1961. In charge of the nursing department, Morag was an efficient, highly organized person who commanded the respect of her co-workers. But Helen found her extremely difficult to work with.

Trans-Atlantic differences could account for some of this. In Britain, nursing sisters hold considerable power and authority, and could even order doctors around if they felt so inclined.

Fortunately, Helen understood that Morag desired the very best for the patients. But they both had their own definite ideas about what kind of treatment they supported for patients and staff and how they expected others to behave in a work setting.

Almost ten years after their first meeting, Helen got word from UMN headquarters that Morag was to be transferred to Amp Pipal. While Helen may have been "soft" on other people, she was also no pushover. She felt so strongly that Morag should not come to Amp Pipal that she took action that surprised even herself. She prepared a tape for the UMN's executive secretary, stating a number of reasons for opposing this staff posting. She based her case mainly on the differences between Canadians and Britons and their incompatibility as co-workers.

The tape sent, she prepared to leave for furlough and stopped en route in Kathmandu. There she made a point of visiting Morag, to learn to her dismay that she had already heard about the tape. "If you don't want me to go to Amp Pipal," Morag told her bluntly, "I won't go."

Morag's flat statement felt like the stab of a knife. Helen immediately regretted sending such a message. Before leaving for Canada she contacted UMN headquarters to tell them to "please ignore everything I said on that tape."

When she returned to Nepal in the fall of 1971, Morag was firmly established as nursing superintendent at Amp Pipal. She had already made significant changes in the operation of the wards and the pharmacy and the medical records department, and had started to train local girls as assistant nurses, a program of vital importance. She made it clear that she planned to make many more changes, in her own way.

Two days after getting back to this "peaceful" setting, Helen found herself in tears. Morag had admittedly done many good things for the hospital, but they had entirely different approaches on how to go about making these changes. It was "the attitude and tone of voice" that upset Helen more than anything, and in the coming months their tensions remained unresolved. The heavy load of patients weighed on them, as they both carried major administrative responsibilities.

They both knew they should have set aside time for consultation and the exchange of ideas, but Helen claimed, legitimately, that she was too busy. She continually had to brush off requests for a meeting with her nursing superintendent. There were just too many patients waiting to be seen at the clinic. Major decisions were constantly deferred until after hours, when both hardworking women were physically and emotionally exhausted.

A year later, when Morag moved from Amp Pipal, she left an invaluable legacy. Her gifts as a capable organizer and administrator had proven essential in getting the fledgling hospital off on the right foot.

It took Helen some time to appreciate fully all that Morag had accomplished. Several years later, when Morag returned to Nepal for a short-term assignment, Helen sent a note of apology ahead and walked down to meet her in Kathmandu. Helen told her how sorry she felt for those unhappy times at Amp Pipal and asked for forgiveness.

But Morag would tolerate no apologies. "Oh, Helen," she said, locking an arm around her waist. "We had so much fun and so many good times together in those days. Just forget all that other stuff."

So Helen did.

29

Unlikely Sisters

One Saturday morning in November, 1988, the Amp Pipal Christian community ended up holding an open-air church service. No one had remembered to bring the key to the church building, so the adults and children settled down on the grassy slope outside.

The assembled group of Nepalis and Westerners sang a few hymns, and after a prayer a short Nepali woman wearing a brown polka-dotted sari with a dark-coloured blouse stood up and turned around to face her friends.

Through thick glasses, she looked directly at each individual before opening her Nepali Bible to Psalm 90. She read a few verses confidently and clearly. "Teach us to number our days, that we may present to Thee a heart of wisdom. . . . Satisfy us in the morning with thy loving kindness, that we may sing for joy and be glad all our days. . . . Let the favour of the Lord our God be upon us." Then she prayed for

God's blessing on the reading of His word and sat down again on the grass, slightly out of breath.

The small, confident woman was Tata, Dr. Helen's cook, house-keeper, laundrywoman, flower-gardener and overall friend for over twenty-five years. Apart from Helen's furlough periods, she worked for Helen since 1964. The employer-employee relationship has long since vanished and they consider themselves more like two sisters.

Two less likely-looking sisters there could not possibly be. Tata is as short and stocky as Helen is tall and lithe. One is dark-skinned, the other fair; one brown-eyed, the other blue.

But they're a good match. Tata's wit and sense of humour are equal to Helen's. The pot is not boiling, Tata corrects Helen, insisting for the thousandth time that it is the water in the pot that is boiling.

"Yes, yes, I know, Tata," says her amused friend. "But would you mind getting the tea ready? The pot's boiling."

Except for the happy ending, Tata's story follows a pattern that is not unusual for a woman in rural Nepal. She was born and raised in Amp Pipal by a mother who was abandoned by her husband and left to raise her young children alone.

Plagued throughout her childhood with a distressing cough and wheezing, Tata was considered frail and had never been given an opportunity to get any education.

When she was about twelve, her mother sent her to be the fourth wife of a man in the neighbouring village of Taku. From his other three wives (the first was Tata's oldest sister), four sons had been born and all died. He was getting older, and Tata was needed to give him a living son before his death.

Barely out of childhood herself, Tata did give him a son, but the infant died soon after birth. Her husband took his anger and disap-pointment out on his girl-wife, and after two weeks of being beaten, starved and abused, she ran away.

Most women had no choice but to return to an abusive home, but Tata was fortunate enough to find work. She was hired by Sodemba, one of the teachers in Jonathan's school back in 1958, and then as a domestic for the family of Howard and Betty Barclay. From them she first saw the love of Jesus displayed, and heard that she too was loved.

She enrolled in night school for illiterate adults and found it hard going but was determined to keep moving through the grade levels.

Every week she attended prayer and Bible study groups led by two UMN women and, fully aware of the consequences, gave her life to Jesus and was baptized in 1961.

When the new lady doctor came to Amp Pipal, Tata went to see her about her coughing. Dr. Helen diagnosed a chronic bronchial condition and prescribed treatment which controlled, but never quite managed to cure, Tata's breathing problem.

Helen needed a reliable housekeeper and Tata, with a wealth of experience in the homes of other mission families, came highly recommended as a cheerful and dependable worker.

One day not long after the new hospital opened, Tata got word of the death of her husband whom she had left years before. Relatives from Taku village came to get her to take part in the *kiriya* (Hindu funeral rites).

Tata knew well the price that others had paid for flouting this Hindu tradition. But she had long since made up her mind that she would not compromise her Christian beliefs.

When the relatives arrived at Amp Pipal, they found no one at Tata's home nor at her work, and none of the neighbours could tell them where to find her. They waited for most of the day, and as dusk was settling and after all the relatives had left to return to Taku, Tata emerged from the corn field that had been her hide-out all day.

Nepali tradition required a newly widowed woman to stay out of public view for six weeks. If any male relative happened to see Tata during that period he would have to do special Hindu *puja*, a time-consuming and costly purification ritual.

For Tata, who walked to work, it meant getting up before dawn and heading down the mountain by a steeper, less-travelled path, and returning the same way after darkness fell. It took courage to walk alone at night; Nepalis are raised in fear and

The irrepressible Tata.

149

dread of darkness, partly from superstition and partly because of the very real danger of walking in pitch black along steep paths.

Tata rarely talks about the unhappiness of the past any more. But sometimes her past confronts her. When her older sister and her sister's children meet her on a path, they refuse to speak to her. She still hears accusations that she jeopardized the salvation of her husband.

Tata says she would never have grown as a Christian without Helen's example and help. And Helen says she never could have worked as long and as hard as she did without Tata's aid and support. She describes her as "one hundred percent honest" and trustworthy, possessing "a heart of gold" that can't help but share food with others who don't have it. In Helen's little thatched house, innumerable guests have feasted on Tata's homemade bread or legendary lemon pudding.

Tata had seen Helen's low periods over the years—times of sadness when there were serious illnesses or difficulties in the hospital, problems in the missionary family, or troubles in the church. At those times, Helen often leaned on Tata, and together they would turn to Jesus for help and guidance.

To little avail, Tata tries to get Helen to rest more and take better care of herself. She says of Helen, "She tries to give the best care for the patients and doesn't care for herself; she worries and doesn't look after herself properly."

The backgrounds of Helen Huston from Alberta, Canada, and Tata from a village in Nepal, could not possibly have been more different. But their futures in eternity will be the same. And in the years between their past and their glorious future, these two women from opposite ends of the world can say to each other, "My sister. My friend."

30

Chandra's Story

Every day, the urgent crowded out the important. A constant stream of people needed patching and repairing, and there was no time left for preventive medicine.

As medical superintendent of the Gorkha Project, Helen gave her report on the year's progress: *"Our help to people around is spotty. Many people are underfed and underclothed. Many of the poorest do not come for help. Few toilets are built and fewer used. Hookworm and amoeba debilitate many. Many water supplies are grossly inadequate and some are badly contaminated."*

Trekkers and mountain climbers could delight in the spectacular scenery, but every day of the year Helen and her nurses looked into the eyes of malnourished children and sickly adults. They had burned themselves out, knowing that they would never make dramatic or lasting changes to the health of the community without a concerted effort at preventive medicine.

It took a five-year-old boy named Chandra to jolt them into action. Chandra's father, Shankar, a dark-haired man about forty years old and a member of the Chettri caste, lived in the remote and primitive village of Lapsibot, a hard fourteen-hour walk to the nearest road. It could have happened to any Nepali child, but this is Chandra's story as told by his father and translated from Nepali:

I live in Lapsibot, at the foot of Mt. Himal Chuli. I grow rice and corn and have a buffalo, two cows and a few goats. I have six children—three boys and three girls.

Chandra, my second youngest, almost five years old, helped his big sister, Kanchi, graze the cows and the buffalo, but he really wanted to go to school with his brothers. One day he got sick.

He had a fever and felt weak and couldn't eat his rice. I wasn't too worried, because there was always someone with fever and cough or dissa lagyo *[diarrhea] in Lapsibot.*

But the next day he got sicker, and his mother, Nirmala, made some lentil soup for him. His throat was so sore he couldn't drink it all and we noticed his breathing was getting worse.

I was out in the yard tying up bundles of corn to dry and could hear him wheezing inside the house. I ran inside and saw him just lying there, hardly breathing. I thought a bit and decided to run and get the jankri *[witch doctor].*

The jankri *came back with me and told me to take Chandra outside and put him on the porch. He asked for two chickens to sacrifice, and he sprinkled the blood all around my boy. Then he picked up his drum and marched around Chandra, thumping and banging and shouting. This was the best way to drive out the* jaasu *[evil spirit] causing him to be sick.*

But Chandra didn't get better; he got worse, and every breath was a struggle. So I thought about carrying him to the new mission hospital. I didn't know what to expect there and felt scared because an old man from the village had gone there for medicine and had died. But two others who had been coughing up blood went and got better. They said there was nothing to be afraid of. The bideshi *[foreigners] in the hospital had been kind to them.*

So I carried Chandra in my arms on the uphill trail, and my second boy, Prem, walked with me, carrying rice, an umbrella and a small bundle of bedding. I knew it would take the whole day and the last part would be hard work, going up and down two lots of steep hills.

Chandra felt hot against my chest and lay limp in my arms. I wondered if he would just stop breathing before we reached the hospital. We stopped for a few minutes' rest only once, by the village water tap at Harmi.

It was dark when we got to Amp Pipal. I thought I would have to ask for directions to the hospital, but soon after, I heard its noise. It made a terrible banging, like the rice-polishing machine in our village, but much louder. Prem asked a man what the noise was, and he said it was the machine for making bijuli [electricity].

We walked down the path a little farther and suddenly saw the outline of a big building with some bright lights. We stopped to rest at the chautara beside it, because I felt so frightened. I was very afraid to go in, but because Chandra was so sick, I walked down the steps to the hospital door.

I felt less frightened right away, when someone from my own country came up to me in a little room and asked if she could help. Then she saw my boy in my arms and ran off. Very quickly she came running back with a foreign lady doctor who said "namaste" [greetings] to greet me and then quickly opened Chandra's shirt to look at him. Then she told the nurse-aide to get ready to do an operation right away. She said there was no time to be lost, but she must have known how I felt because she sat down beside me for a few minutes and talked in my own language about everything she was going to do.

She said something was blocking Chandra's breathing. They would have to operate to make a hole in the front of his windpipe so he could breathe, but his chances were not good.

I felt better to hear what the trouble was. Even if it was bad news, it was comforting when she spoke. She asked if I agreed to the operation and I put my thumbprint on a piece of paper.

Then she put her hand on Chandra's forehead and asked if it would be all right to pray for him, to pray that he would get better. I knew she would be talking to the Christian God but said yes anyway. Our Hindu gods hadn't helped.

Then they took Chandra away and Prem and I squatted down on the floor and waited and ate some of our chiura [pounded rice]. The way my boy looked, I didn't think he would survive. We who live in Lapsibot have seen enough of sick children, and I have already lost three of my own. It's a fact of life, that's all.

After the operation they brought Chandra back to us, and we could see that his fingernails and lips had changed from blue back to pink. He looked so much better, but he couldn't talk because of the tube in his windpipe. He could only make signs. The lady doctor in the white coat came to see him every day and held his hand and told him he was getting better.

I wondered where she had come from and why she had come to Nepal, but I was afraid to ask her. She always seemed to be busy. Probably she was working to help poor people like us in order to get karma [merit] in the next life. Why should people who worship the Christian God be any different from us?

A few days later Chandra was able to drink buffalo milk and to eat soft rice. He sat up in bed and the nurses moved his bed outside where he could lie in the sun. I asked Dr. Helen when I could take him home. She told me not yet, but perhaps in a couple of days.

But the next day was terrible. Prem and I were standing by Chandra's bed when he suddenly turned blue and seemed to pass out. The nurse and doctor came quickly, and we moved to the side while they tried to get him breathing again, but he just lay there, white and still.

The doctor turned to look at me and said, in a voice so soft I could hardly hear, "Maph garnos" [I'm sorry]. Her eyes looked very sad. You would have thought it was her son who had just died.

I had nothing to say. I had been through this before.

Prem and I wrapped Chandra in a cotton cloth the hospital gave us. I carried him in my arms down the hill to the river. It was only an hour's walk, but when we reached the river bank I felt so tired, far more tired than after the long walk from Lapsibot. We bought firewood from a farmer and then laid the boy on top. I didn't have money to pay for a Brahmin priest, so we lit the fire ourselves, and then we looked away from it and watched the black smoke drift across the river. Soon it was all over. Prem and I threw the embers and ashes into the river.

Before leaving for home, we stopped at the hospital to get our bundle of clothing and were just about to leave the room when the lady doctor in the white coat came up and told us again how sorry she was. She wondered if we had some food for our long walk home. Then she asked me questions *about my other children at home and wanted to know if any of them had received a sui [injection]. I told her no and started to leave.*

Then she said something that made me stop and turn around. I could hardly believe it. Prem asked if what she said was really true.

"Yes, it is true," she told us. "If Chandra had been given an injection when he was a baby, he would never have got this terrible disease. He would be alive today. You have other small children at home that you love. Take them to a health post or bring them to this hospital for the injections they need."

I didn't say anything. I always thought that really bad sickness was caused by evil spirits or witches. Could an injection scare off an evil spirit? It's hard for me to know what to do. Maybe I should listen to the tall lady doctor in the white coat.

Little Chandra had lost his life to a complication of diphtheria that affects the heart. Diphtheria was one of the preventable diseases that struck down scores of children, along with whooping cough, measles, tetanus, polio and smallpox.

But his young life was not lost in vain.

Never again in the Gorkha district would disease-causing germs and viruses be free to spread their contagion unopposed. Battle lines were drawn up and the little hospital in the hills would be in the forefront on the conflict, not just to combat, but more importantly, to prevent illness.

And although the day-to-day struggle against sickness would never cease, the near future would see many of these vicious childhood diseases stopped by a hypodermic needle before they got started.

31

Healing, Teaching and Comforting

It seemed logical to concentrate public health and education efforts at the beginning of life. Statistics bore out the fact that children were the most vulnerable to any health menace. Forty percent of rural Nepali children died before reaching the age of five. Maternal deaths in childbirth were almost as deplorable—850 per 100,000 births, compared to the range of two to ten in Western countries.

The causes were known well enough: sickly mothers, children spaced too closely together, not enough food, no immunization, poor sanitation and absent or poor care.

At Amp Pipal hospital, shocking statistics translated into a stream of real sorrows.

By the time his mother arrived at the hospital with Tika Ram in her arms, he was semi-conscious. A five-year old malnourished boy, he had developed serious complications of measles.

Helen had firsthand experience with the ravages of measles, a disease regarded as a childhood "nuisance" in Canada.

After nourishing tube feedings Tika Ram began to improve, and five days later started to regain consciousness. But his speech was still irrational and he shook and trembled, shouting that buffaloes were going to trample him. His mother trembled even more than he did and screamed that an evil spirit had possessed him. She pleaded with Dr. Helen, even getting down on her knees, to let her take the boy home. The evil spirit could be cast out, she said, only by going through the Hindu *puja* (worship).

Helen sat down on a bench beside the distraught mother. "Please don't take him yet," she urged her. "You can see that he is slowly getting better. His fever is going down and he's no longer unconscious. It would be dangerous to take him home. Do you understand what I am saying?"

The woman nodded her head Nepali style, but Helen knew from the avoided eye contact that her agreement was a polite show. She doubted that she really did understand. Later that evening, when she visited the children's ward, she found that she was right. Tika Ram's cot was empty. His mother had taken him from the hospital to call on a witch doctor.

Families often waited until their children were at the point of death before bringing them to Amp Pipal. It was often several days' walk from home, the trip was costly, and there were no assurances of success. They were more likely to bring a boy than a girl, however, because sons were so highly prized.

Another five-year-old boy with measles was almost beyond hope when his father carried him from their village two hours' walk from the hospital. The boy had survived two major hemorrhages caused by poor blood clotting, one of the rare complications of measles. Twenty minutes after reaching the hospital, the boy bled again and died almost instantly. It was no wonder that Helen called measles a curse.

Many common childhood diseases could be fought successfully if a child were well fed. A nutritionist with the UMN developed several recipes for Nepali-style nutritious formulas, simple preparations that Helen counted on daily and credited with saving innumerable malnourished children and weakened adults. One formula was

157

sorbottam pito, a finely ground porridge mixture of three locally grown grains.

Intestinal worms lived as parasites in almost all villagers. Dakurni Maya was a pretty eight-year-old girl with a complexion as white as the Himalayan "snows." She arrived at the hospital puffing and panting for breath. Hookworms lodging in her digestive system had sucked so much blood that she was seriously anemic.

Dakurni Maya.

Medication eliminated the hookworm easily enough and iron supplements built up her blood. But as long as she continued to work barefoot in muddy rice fields, the hookworm larvae would keep invading through the cleft between the toes, and the cycle would be repeated.

One of the most sinister of all diseases, rabies or hydrophobia struck in mini-epidemics. Bhim Dasarat, a fifteen-year-old boy, was carried to the hospital eight weeks after being bitten by a mad dog. The same free-roaming dog had bitten at least two other people and seven buffaloes, and all had died.

Bhim could still speak when he arrived at Amp Pipal, but all his limbs were paralyzed. His family was taken aside and advised to expect the worst. Twelve hours later he was gone. His life could have been spared had he come to the hospital for a series of vaccine injections after the bite.

It took time for the villagers to understand rabies and the vaccines, but there were signs that the message was getting through. From one village, fifteen people walked a round trip of six hours for fourteen days to get the full treatment of rabies vaccine that would save them from the fate of Bhim Dasarat.

Of all the myriad causes of disease, the drinking of contaminated water was the most common and the most serious. Using precious firewood to boil the water or adding purification tablets were effective methods of making it safe for consumption, but were too costly.

It seemed idealistic but one of the goals of the young hospital aimed to teach every patient something about nutrition, pure water, hygiene and sanitation. Health teaching in the schools expanded to include grades three to eight. Community health developed into a separate hospital-based department and eventually grew to include trained teams of Nepali health workers in their own villages.

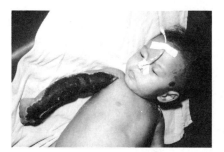

Unusual complication of measles— gangrene. Good response to surgical treatment.

Boy with fractured femur after being carried for three days in a doko on his brother's back.

From its foothold in the hills, the hospital slowly and steadily gained credibility. More and more, the people accepted that tiny living things they couldn't see, called bacteria and viruses, caused their sicknesses, not bad karma or evil spirits that needed to be appeased and feared.

Many curable and preventable diseases have been virtually wiped out in Canada. Tuberculosis, polio, diphtheria, smallpox and typhoid have faded into the past. Effective treatment has knocked out the dangers of childhood pneumonia and diarrhea.

In countries as poor and underdeveloped as Nepal, the situation is vastly different. Canada's problems of yesteryear are the main destroyers of life in the mountain villages of that country. An outbreak of measles in the village of Choprak, three hours' walk from Amp Pipal, took the lives of fourteen children.

Two reasonable meals a day could change the whole picture for young children. Pure drinking water would eliminate an estimated sixty percent of the diseases in rural Nepal. Contaminated water carries, among others, the germs of hepatitis, diarrhea and typhoid fever.

Not a few problems arose from ignorance and superstition. Many an infant with diarrhea died of dehydration because the mother deliberately withheld fluids.

Among the village people some foods were considered hot, or *garmi*, and others cold, *sardi*. You got sick from an imbalance of hot and cold food in your system. Thus a toothache, caused by an excess of cold foods, could be cured by a good dose of homemade whisky, a hot food. One of the most common questions a doctor had to answer was, "What food can I eat?" It paid to know all about hot and cold foods.

Helen and her colleagues faced a formidable task, but the strategy seemed clear—by all means to complete and upgrade the hospital to make it an effective place for curative care. But now she realized it was even more important to teach good health at every opportunity: "We're committed to teach everything we know; to try and do oursleves out of a job."

It was vital to take the message into the community. Better still, work in partnership with the community to promote health care and to prevent the ravages of disease.

It was a time to recall Jonathan's words in praise of health teaching in the classroom, where, for instance, after a 100% incidence among the schoolboys in 1958, scabies and intestinal worms had been practically eliminated.

It was possible.

The words of Frank Wilcox, Executive Secretary of the UMN in 1972 served as a banner proclaiming some of the goals and objectives of the mission:

"... *adequate interpretations of the term 'salvation' include ... 'health' and 'wholeness.'*

"... *Thus it is not simply a kind, humanitarian purpose that the children of Nepal should have a wholesome, nutritious diet; that adequate medical care should be available to all; that education should be every child's privilege.*

"*These are all a real part of God's loving, liberating purpose for all men.*"

*****

Death was no stranger to most Nepali villagers. Familiarity had made them more accepting of its chill reality and more prepared to talk about it and to face it. But few doctors find it easy to talk about

160

dying with their patients and relatives. It's hard to be the bearer of ill tidings and hard to know what to say to a patient who is getting worse day by day.

Helen seemed to feel at ease with the desperately ill. She was able to speak with them, comfort them and nearly always pray with them. In later years this ministry would become a source of peace and comfort to great numbers of people fearful of the "Valley of the Shadow."

During his short stay in Amp Pipal hospital, Ganesh Prasad Joshi, a thin little man in his fifties who had been in failing health for some months, learned that he had an incurable cancer of the lung.

Before being told the bad news, he and his wife and two daughters seemed to be in a very agitated state, as if they suspected something wrong. Ganesh himself slept poorly, developed a tremor and constantly ran outside to smoke a cigarette.

Helen could see that the time had come for him to know the truth. Before doing so, she paused to pray that God would enable her to say the right words and that He would comfort the family. To her surprise, he stopped shaking and the tension lines in his face seemed to relax. He asked Helen many questions.

"Could there be any doubt about my disease?" he asked. "Are you certain that I cannot possibly be cured?"

Helen assured him there was little room for doubt. But his reply surprised her.

"I won't shed a tear and neither will my wife and daughters. But there is one thing you can do for me: please write a letter to my brother-in-law, asking him to care for my family after I have gone. I have a few matters to settle but after that's done, I want to spend my time in worship to God."

Helen realized that his agitation was partly because he hadn't been told the truth and partly because he was not ready for death, although the idea had entered his head. She was deeply moved to hear him speak so confidently and sincerely.

He seemed secure in his Hindu religion but wanted Helen to pray for him to the Christian God. She told him the Good News of Jesus, God's supreme gift to mankind. She did her best to prepare him for the greatest single test that any man has to face—his death.

And she would continue to pray to God for the critically sick, to commit them into His hand, often expecting Him to intervene and

161

bring about a cure. After all, she had once said, is anything too great for the God of the galaxies?

Sometimes answers to her prayers seemed indisputable—such as the woman with meningitis who regained consciousness after half an hour of frantic cardio-pulmonary resuscitation (C.P.R.). She walked home by herself and her family had to dispose of the firewood they had gathered for her cremation.

Then there was the critically ill six-year-old girl, Bimala, who died late in the afternoon of Easter Sunday after much pleading and praying. "I found it quite hard to trust God that He had heard our prayer and done what was best for the wee girl," Helen confided. Was she expecting too much? Her confidence in the power of God to do great things had not wavered over the years. But the loss of a six-year old child made her feel so heavy-hearted.

Had her unshakeable optimism overstepped the bounds of rationality and good sense? At one time Cynthia Hale wondered. She and Helen had shared in the care of Ganga, a thirty-five-year-old woman with severe headaches and seizures due to a suspected brain tumor. Her family had no money to take her elsewhere for treatment and she refused to go, even if treatment were free.

Ganga was the subject of much prayer, by the bedside and elsewhere; on one occasion, Helen gathered a group of seven people to pray for Ganga. She expressed confidence that He could and would cure her of the life-threatening disease.

Ganga and her husband began to ask about Jesus. He had healed lame beggars, people with leprosy, and blind persons while he walked the dusty roads of Galilee. Ganga smiled more easily, but the headaches did not relent. Then she lost her speech and developed hemiplegia (paralysis of one side). When Ganga's husband asked to take her home, Helen agreed to let her go, still optimistic that she would get better.

A month later the news reached Amp Pipal hospital: Ganga lapsed into a coma and died at home.

Her fervent prayer had gone unanswered. And the mystery would never really be cleared up until she herself took the same journey as Ganga and little Bimala.

162

32

Tek Bahadur

Helen had seen plenty of reasons for people not to become Christians, beginning with her visits in 1961 to believers locked up like common criminals in the foul Tansen jail.

And the Nepali Christians from Amp Pipal and everywhere else needed all the encouragement and nurturing they could get. They lived in a hostile and unforgiving environment.

Prem (not his real name), a tall, muscular man about thirty-five, lived with his wife and family in a village high up in the hills above Amp Pipal. One day Helen received a letter about Prem from a UMN colleague working nearby. The village had condemned Prem for being a Christian and made him an outcast. The letter went on:

"... *they cannot help anyone in the village and no one is allowed to work for them. They are not to receive any meat ever from the village and cannot sit or visit with anyone ... the kids will not be allowed any contact with the other kids. Prem's wife is taking a lot of abuse from her brother.*

"Please pray for them—that despite all this they manage to stay cheerful and strong in the Lord."

Orthodox Hinduism still held a tight grip on most villagers. They accepted the help of the hospital and the great benefits of the United Mission projects but at the same time resented anything they considered a challenge to their religion.

For most, the cost of becoming a Christian was just too high a price to pay. They could face beatings, jailings and court cases and would almost certainly be slandered, threatened and—the worst blow—denied access to the communal water supply.

If they were attracted to "the missionaries' religion" because they expected practical advantages in the form of good jobs or scholarships, they were soon disillusioned. These "rice-Christians" turned back when they found hardships instead.

But some remained faithful and stuck it out, saying that the new freedom and forgiveness found in Jesus was worth far more than abuse and suffering. No longer did they live in fear of witches and evil spirits and the need to be constantly placating a pantheon of Hindu gods.

The welfare of her fellow believers assumed a top priority for Helen. As Jagat Maya said, "If the believers were firm and growing [in the faith], Helen was happy. If not, she was saddened, somtimes weeping if they were falling away, or perplexed."

Her role was to support, encourage, sometimes advise and always to pray but not to lead. The church must not bear her imprint: it must be indigenous, based on the Bible but born in the hills of Nepal.

Nurturing and encouraging the local church over the years was not without its disappointments and heartaches. Helen wrote about this to her friends in her 1975 Christmas letter:

"In some ways the church in Nepal is growing; in other ways, weak and poor. For some, the stigma of being a Christian has been too much to bear and they've gone back into nominal Hinduism. . . .

"Nepali Christian leaders are few, but some are godly, mature men and women."

Tek Bahadur Bhandary's early life had looked so promising. As a child, he stood at the top of class five when his father died; he had to quit school to help his family.

At the age of nineteen misfortune struck. While he worked high up on a tree cutting twigs for goat fodder, a branch broke and he fell. He lay on the ground unable to get up. He couldn't move or feel his legs. Villagers carried him to Amp Pipal hospital in a *doli*.

He accepted the doctor's verdict the way most Nepali accept news, good or bad: his face and eyes showed no emotion. He asked questions in a quiet, business-like manner. Would he ever be able to walk again? Was his life in danger? Was there any hope?

He was not spared the truth: his spinal cord had been crushed and his legs would never bear his weight again. His life was very much in danger—pressure sores and bladder infection would likely finish him off in a year or two. In the hills of Nepal, traumatic paraplegia, as it was called, was incompatible with life.

Tek Bahadur sank into a black pit of depression. His family soon stopped coming to feed and care for him and he had only one wish left: to die.

But the hospital staff did not give up on him. They wouldn't stop caring. They showed him how to turn in bed to avoid pressure sores in the paralyzed area and encouraged him to eat and to read. They instructed him how to empty his bladder. He made progress but couldn't shake the despair. Other patients came and went but Tek stayed, wondering if he would be a permanent fixture in the men's ward.

In the meantime, the hospital administration was also wondering what to do with Tek. Hospital beds were always full. They couldn't keep him indefinitely. They prayed for a solution, and the answer came from a Canadian woman named Isobel Clark.

Many years before, a seriously ill two-year-old boy named Will Huston had been a patient of Isobel's father. When the boy grew a little older, he looked after the doctor's horse and did chores for

Dr. Huston examining the paralyzed Tek Bahadur.

165

him during the summers. The two Ontario families became close friends.

Isobel Clark had planned a memorial for her father but changed her mind and decided to send the money to the hospital in Nepal where Will Huston's daughter had been working for thirteen years.

Isobel's gift was just enough to finance an important project, the construction of a small private room at one side of the hospital—a home for Tek Bahadur. The stone addition was built with a large window and a private entrance.

Now, bolstered by having his own room and encouraged by everyone who came near him, Tek Bahadur emerged from his despair. He mastered typing in both Nepali and English, learned to cook his own food and began to travel around the hospital in a wheelchair that Helen had bought for him on one of her trips back from Canada. Then he offered to work as a volunteer in the hospital records office.

Puzzled by these Christians who hadn't given up on him, Tek began to ask questions. Who was this Jesus they talked to? How could he know more about Him? And finally, how could he become a Christian?

The decision to turn to Jesus changed Tek Bahadur's life. Still bound to his wheelchair, he said he now felt as free as a bird, and his gloom had changed to joy. Although only half of his body functioned, he was prepared to offer it and his heart and his mind to the Lord, and he wanted to be baptized.

"People here will find out," warned the leader of the Amp Pipal church. "Your own family may hate you. They may disown you. Do you still want to go ahead?"

Tek answered, "Yes, I don't care what they may say."

Pastor Daud added a final warning. "You may have to go to jail for three years. Are you still willing?"

Said Tek, "I am ready."

True to his word, he was ready. After baptism, he moved straight ahead, to become a keen scholar of the Bible, an active member of the Amp Pipal church (carried up the hill in his wheelchair by three strong men) and, later, a member of the church committee. His slender face, wide and friendly brown eyes and quiet and confident manner compelled attention when he was called upon to expound truths from the Bible during church services.

He began working for the hospital's records and cashier's office as a volunteer and learned so quickly that he was soon a full member of the staff. He took on responsible jobs in patient registration and accounting. Before and after work, he moved smoothly about the wards in his wheelchair, visiting and encouraging patients.

He learned about Isobel, the Doctor's daughter and Will Huston and one day in 1976 typed a letter to Will.

"... I was obliged for your kindness, prayer, because I am so blessed.

"... As my spiritual life is still young and green and my faith not strong enough. ...

"How glad a thing that Canada and Nepal, we together, fellowship with prayer. I am very thankfully. ..."

Tek Bahadur Bhandary.

33

The Blue Tibetan Dress

The official letter of notification had reached Kathmandu on May 11, 1978, sending a ripple of excitement through the ranks of her UMN colleagues. Dr. Helen Huston was to receive the Outstanding Achievement Award from the Medical Alumni Association of the University of Alberta. Never before had this honour been bestowed on a missionary-doctor. And never had an award winner been chosen on the basis of accomplishments outside of clinical or research work.

My wife Alison and I were doubly excited because the University of Alberta was also our alma mater, and Helen and I had graduated together. Our lives had rarely come into contact with Helen's until we joined the UMN in 1974 and I worked as a surgeon in Kathmandu. Our friendship with Helen grew, although we were still separated by the all-day journey to Amp Pipal.

The only UMNer who remained quite indifferent to the announcement was the award's recipient. Helen's complete lack of enthusiasm extended to such essential matters as planning the clothes she would wear for the official ceremony in Edmonton in September.

Although she carried herself with elegance, her wardrobe was highly unimpressive. It consisted of white dresses and jackets for work, a few rather tired-looking blouses, some shaggy sweaters and long skirts. Because of unusually high arches, she couldn't wear the rubber sandals that many Nepalis wore. Instead she opted for well-worn leather hiking boots, padded with a double layer of thick woollen socks when she set out for a long trek.

As soon as they heard about the impending award ceremony, three UMN friends, Mia Voreland from Norway, Doris Bailey and Alison Hankins, both from Canada, did a little detective work and found out that Helen was planning to wear an ancient sari. She had bought it in India years before and had stored it in a drawer at home in Canada.

The sari would never do, the friends agreed. Even if it weren't so old, saris are not particularly flattering to tall women, and of course Helen had never bothered to get a proper fit.

In the true spirit of conspiracy, they made a decision without Helen's knowledge or approval: she would wear a dress that would make her look positively regal. It would be a Tibetan dress.

Via the Kathmandu–Amp Pipal mail-running route, the trio somehow managed to secure Helen's grudging agreement to have a Tibetan dress tailor-made—as long as it didn't cost too much.

Then followed discussion of the design, and much the way mothers pore over patterns for a daughter's wedding dress, Mia, Dorothy and Alison chose a design for a simple, floor-length, sleeveless gown with a V-shaped neckline, a close fitting bodice and a narrow belt around the waist.

They sent several swatches of fabric to Amp Pipal for Helen's approval. She chose an attractive blue which was their preference also, but refused to accept their recommendation of the brocade and insisted upon a cheaper rayon.

When the last stitch was tied, the blue Tibetan dress looked magnificent. A white blouse with a rolled collar would show it off to perfection. All three conspirators smiled and nodded in approval.

At a price of three hundred rupees (about thirty Canadian dollars) for materials and labour, it was definitely a bargain. But they had good reason to figure that Helen, who cared little about clothes, would probably be outraged. So before the final tally was sent to her in Amp Pipal, there were major downward adjustments to the bottom line.

*****

Helen left for furlough in Canada during the summer. Alison and I followed soon after. Around noon on Friday, September 22, 1978, Alison and I left Calgary, Alberta, for the drive to Edmonton for the annual meeting and banquet of the Medical Alumni Association of our old university. The Alberta countryside glowed with the soft golden colours of autumn. Combines were cutting wide swathes through fields of ripened grain; into the boxes of three-ton trucks poured the season's bounty of barley and canola. I found my thoughts drifting back to the Nepali farmer cutting every stalk of rice with his *hansiya* (sickle) and then flailing the dried bundles against the ground.

At the Plaza Hotel in Edmonton, it wasn't hard to pick Helen out of the throng. Looking like a queen in her blue Tibetan dress, she was surrounded by a crowd. She appeared relaxed and filled with fun as though this was her usual setting for a Friday evening.

I thought she looked great, but Alison immediately noticed something was not right. She edged close to Helen's side, and after a lot of whispering back and forth, and a wide-eyed look from Helen, I watched the two of them move away from the crowd and disappear behind a big potted plant. A few minutes later their laughing faces reappeared, before switching instantly to a convincing composure.

By my side again, Alison saw my quizzical look. "It's okay now," she explained. "She had the waistbands on her new dress tied wrong, at the back. I had to untie them and bring them around to the front. She does look lovely, doesn't she?"

We watched her as she stood beside her sister Mary, who had come from Phoenix, Arizona, for the occasion. Then we noticed her father, Will Huston, at eighty-three, neatly dressed and very sharp looking. This evening, he told us, ranked as one of the highlights of his life.

Three other fellow workers from the UMN, Doris Bailey and Mike and Annette Boorman from Rimbey, the little Alberta town where Will Huston had pastored forty years before, were also present. Mike had worked a term as an anesthetist at Shanta Bhawan Hospital.

Dr. Alton presents the Outstanding Achievement Award to Helen.

The ceremony began. Dr. Macgregor Alton, President of the M.A.A. and a former classmate of Helen and me, called everyone into the banquet hall. Head table guests, ushered in by a handsome Scottish piper, included Dean Cameron of the Faculty of Medicine, Alex Markle of the Alumni Association and, of course, Helen Huston.

After the dinner, a nudge from Mac Alton prompted me into action. It was my honour to introduce to the large gathering Dr. Helen Huston, my colleague and friend. As she stepped forward in her blue Tibetan dress, the room exploded into applause. I stayed on my feet to join the spontaneous, cheering standing ovation.

And then the microphone was hers.

She gave an inspired address. She began by saying that she was happy to accept the award, but only on behalf of all medical doctors who work quietly in the shadows, where they are most needed, without expecting any acclaim.

Then she talked about her adopted country and her adopted friends—about Bir Bahadur with TB of the lungs, about Kanchi who had lost so many babies, about Chandra who died because he had never been innoculated. She introduced her audience to Jagat, Annama, Nanu Maya and other Nepali staff upon whom the medical work depended so heavily.

She called for lights to be dimmed and showed a few slides—scenes of the magnificent scenery of Nepal, the little hospital in the hills, a few of the workers she had spoken of and some of the patients she had treated. At the end she spoke about the goodness of God and the wonderful privilege He had given her, to serve Him as a doctor in Nepal.

She sat down, but had to get up again to accept from President Alton the scroll bearing the citation, "In recognition of distinguished service in Medicine, the Medical Alumni Association of the University of Alberta proudly presents the Outstanding Achievement Award for 1978 to . . ." that called for another standing ovation.

When we left the banquet just before midnight, the guest of honour in the blue Tibetan dress was still standing at the front shaking hands. We caught her eye and waved goodbye. We'd be seeing her soon in the hills of Nepal.

Helen with her proud father.

34
Helen Didi

The decade of the seventies brought changes to the little country of Nepal, changes beginning with the monarchy. When King Mahendra died from a heart attack in 1974, his son, Crown Prince Birendra succeeded him.

Many foreign organizations entered the country to assist in nation-wide development. The People's Republic of China built a 200-kilometre road from Kathmandu to Pokhara and a trolley bus route over the nineteen kilometres from Kathmandu to Bhaktapur. Canadian aid supplied, among other things, several Twin Otter airplanes and training of pilots for the domestic air service.

Yet the Nepalis, known for their independence and strong cultural identity, refused to get swallowed up or swept up in all the trappings of development.

Admittedly the face of the cities, Kathmandu in particular, changed but life remained as before for the villager and the farmer in his rice field. And for Amp Pipal and neighbouring villages like Harmi, Borogaon and Sano Dumri—all without electricity and sewage disposal and hours walk from any road—national development, so called, seemed light years away.

Since arriving in the Gorkha District in 1960, Helen had immersed herself completely in the Nepal scene, calling Amp Pipal her home. Over the years the UMN had called her to relieve other doctors for short periods, but she always came back to the little hospital in the hills.

Canada could lay claim to being her native land but Nepal meant even more. God had called her to this distant corner of His vineyard where she would spend nearly all her working years.

And she loved the country: the craggy, white mountains; the warm monsoon rains; the green hills and the scarlet poinsettia bushes; the white egrets and the dazzling yellow sunbirds.

Most of all she loved the people. She had cared for thousands of them, sometimes seeing them at times of deepest crisis, and she loved them all, from proud Brahmins all the way down to the lowly unwashed Sarki caste. She loved even those who were impossible to like—the complaining, the dirty and the dishevelled, the demanding and obnoxious. It made no difference.

And this love found expression in the care she gave her patients. Dr. Del Haug, medical director during 1980s, expressed it well:

"She had little thought for her own comfort, spending long hours in the Outpatient Department and invariably arriving home late for supper. She agonized over the really sick patients. Frequently she would walk down to the hospital late at night to check on them again, and often to pray with and for them."

The Nepalis reciprocated her love. For numberless people living in those green hills Helen epitomized the Amp Pipal hospital and the service it had given to the community. They called her "Helen Didi," a name of respect and affection translated as "older sister Helen."

Once, after recovering from an illness, Helen was walking with Maya Holbrook from the hospital up to the bazaar on the Amp Pipal ridge. Maya, wife of Canadian agriculturist Norman Holbrook, later said that virtually everyone they met on the path stopped and asked about Helen. It took a whole hour to complete the usual twenty minute walk.

Many villagers even thought she possessed miraculous powers of healing, an attitude she abhorred.

Children were drawn to her, like cedar waxwings to a mountain ash tree. When out walking, she sometimes taught simple action songs to the children clustering around her; at one time "so many were following me around that I felt like a pied piper," she wrote.

Young Shobba Gurung, Nursing Superintendent from 1982 onward, cried when she first came to isolated Amp Pipal from busy Kathmandu. But the strangeness and the loneliness faded over the next few days when she met "Dr. Helen who treated me as if I were her daughter." Shobha's husband, curly-haired Iman, appreciated the way Helen sought his opinion about plans and developments in the O.R. where he worked as supervisor.

Nanu Maya, an attractive woman in her late thirties, was baptized as a Christian at the age of fifteen. One of the more fortunate local Amp Pipal girls, she had managed to pass Class Eight. She subsequently completed her schooling before taking nurses training at Shanta Bhawan.

A woman of unflinching faith in the face of much opposition, she became the leader in the local church and a solid performer on the wards. She spoke about Helen in her own language:

"I have the highest regard for Dr. Helen. She has encouraged and assisted me and countless others, in many ways, not just in the faith. She delights, above all else, in being the servant of the Lord. . . .

"She is respected and admired far and wide. In fact, many patients are not happy unless they can see Dr. Helen."

The nation's respect and gratitude for Helen and her long-term service to the people of Nepal culminated in a unique award by the Nepal Medical Association at the annual conference in the Bir Hospital, Kathmandu in February, 1980.

The Prime Minister of Nepal, Surya Bahadur Thapa, at a special ceremony presented Dr. Helen Huston with a scroll containing her Honorary Life Membership in the N.M.A. Never before had such an honour been granted to a doctor from a foreign country.

It meant that Helen would never again have to pay annual dues to the N.M.A. But that didn't get her off the hook for dues in arrears for the previous two years!

They must have forgiven her, for in 1991 the Nepal Medical Association presented another award for her "extraordinary contribution in the medical and health sector."

35

Patience with Patients

Byron Christopher, an Edmonton reporter, faced a most challenging assignment—to travel to Nepal and write an article on Dr. Helen Huston and her work at the hospital in the clouds. He would need to hike up the hills to Amp Pipal and spend a week with her there interviewing and taking pictures.

Before Byron left, Helen said she wanted him to return to Canada remembering that missionaries, herself included, are very ordinary people.

"You've seen my holes and weaknesses. . . ."

"I meant it when I said how easy it is for me to be irritable, critical and unkind. Where is His gentleness?

"You stayed around long enough to see we're ordinary run-of-the-mill people. . . ."

"She's the most beautiful Christian I have ever known," said Dr. Tom Hale, who called it "the greatest joy and privilege" to work with her. He also called her "the most conscientious doctor I have ever seen."

Sometimes that painstaking conscientiousness could be frustrating for Tom because it meant extra work for him. Working as a team, they had to put in long hours getting through the line-up in the out-patient clinic, and if Helen took extra time with patients, the line stayed long. Why can't she make up her mind? he often wondered.

When it came to psychiatric patients, the harmony was stretched to the limit. Tom didn't like to see beds taken up for long periods by neurotic or psychotic patients, and almost invariably these patients were admitted by Helen.

The mentally deranged sometimes disrupted the hospital routine and disturbed other patients by breaking windows, throwing food around the wards or screaming during the nights.

One of these special patients of Helen broke down the door of the men's ward one night and proceeded to tear his mattress to shreds. The next morning, the two doctors were doing their ward rounds separately and happened to meet at the scene of the destruction.

Tom surveyed the damage and began to whistle softly. "Well, doctor," he said, raising his eyebrows. "Am I right in assuming that this patient's treatment is nearly finished and he's ready to go home?"

Helen wasn't slow at picking up the thinly disguised hint, and throwing back her head, she broke into her well-known laugh. "I'm really terribly sorry about the mess, Tom," she answered, getting in the last word, "but I'm sure you'll agree that patients are more important than mattresses."

Tom couldn't argue with that remark.

They needed these times when they could laugh together—and sometimes at each other.

One day Helen got a tin of coconut in the mail and decided to make a batch of cookies. She had always enjoyed cooking, and on this day she and a friend, pediatrician Dr. Eleanor Knox, baked over a hundred cookies, not an easy feat on a wood stove.

The finished cookies were a disaster, about as hard and tasteless as fossilized cardboard. Something had certainly gone wrong. Scratching their heads, the two cooks sat down and were on the point of performing an autopsy on one of the cookies when they heard a knock on the door. It was Tom.

"Something sure smells good," said Tom after he had been invited to come in.

"We've been making coconut cookies," said Helen, with a furtive sideways glance at Eleanor, "like to try one?"

Tom accepted the invitation. Just then the two ladies found something else to do. With his strong incisor teeth Tom managed to bite into one of the cookies and then began to chew. Struggling hard, he managed to get it down.

A moment later Helen approached with a plateful. "Like another?" she asked.

Tom managed a weak smile. "Maybe later on," he suggested.

Then he saw Eleanor's raised eyebrow and realized he had been trapped.

He suddenly exploded with laughter, picking up one of the offending cookies and threatening to throw it at the schemers. "Okay, you got me this time," he said, "but I have ways and means of getting even, you know. Better watch out next time you come to our house for supper!"

While Tom and Cynthia often laughed together with Helen, they shared times of sadness and heaviness, too. And sometimes there were tears.

Helen was at a village two to three hours' walk from Amp Pipal the day a young man was brought in to the hospital with serious abdominal injuries. He had slipped and fallen from the roof of his house and needed emergency surgery. Tom immediately sent the patient's brother to run with a message to his colleague. It was noon when Helen made it back to the hospital and prepared to anesthetize the patient.

She put a breathing tube down the young man's windpipe and kept him asleep with ether. Tom found two holes in the intestine and after repairing both, was sewing up the incision when Helen suddenly became alarmed. The boy's blood pressure was dropping, and before the doctors could respond he turned blue and his heart stopped beating.

Tom and Helen quickly searched and found the cause. The tube in his windpipe had kinked and blocked off his airway. They straightened the kink and worked hard to get air to the oxygen-starved boy, but it was too late. Their young patient died on the operating table.

Tom had the painful task of breaking the news to the young man's family waiting in the corridor. Then he turned into the little office outside the operating room and found Helen sitting at the desk. Her head was bowed, her chin rested on clasped hands, and her cheeks were wet.

There was no consolation in knowing that the tube was an old one, less rigid than it should have been. That didn't matter. The life and safety of the young man had rested in her hands—and she had let him down.

36

Buddhiman Bahadur— A Leprosy Friend

The first of a long series of foreign medical students began to arrive in the mountain hospital for "elective periods," designed to give them experience in Third World medicine. Many were profoundly affected by the example set at Amp Pipal hospital.

One British medical student, now a UMN doctor in Nepal with his wife and four young children, said watching Helen's life changed his mind about the difference one person could make in so vast a need. "Helen Huston proved to me that our lives can make a difference," he said. "That's why I'm in Nepal and not in a country that has more than enough of everything."

July, 1975 set the stage for the role that Helen would occupy for years to come, namely, as the senior member of a team under the leadership of someone else. Her non-medical duties now consisted of liason officer with UMN headquarters, chairperson of the housing committee and care of the social and spiritual welfare of the staff.

Insofar as plans and budgets, management and administrative hassles were concerned, she was off the hook.

It was freeing, in a sense, but there was a price to pay. She possessed a vast experience, and a fair measure of wisdom, but henceforth she would be called upon to accept the decisions and plans of the current medical director. As Dr. Tim Linton of Australia was to say of her some time later, "She is keen to be an active member of the team, without directing the traffic."

The new arrangement allowed her to focus on her over-riding concern—patient care. She would do all in her power to be the best possible doctor for each patient crossing the threshold of her doorway. In spite of her constant companion, "irresolution," her advice was often sought by Tom and Cynthia and other medical associates for help in making a diagnosis in bizarre or obscure cases. One of her medical colleagues called her abilities "awesome."

The spectrum of diseases never ceased to amaze her. One day in 1975 she made a list of patients under her care:

- A seventeen-year-old boy with a badly infected compound fracture of his lower leg. He arrived at the hospital six days after his injury.
- An eighteen-month-old baby with second degree burns of the buttocks. (Burns of children were still very common, as open fire pits were used for cooking and heating.)
- An eighteen-year-old married girl with far advanced TB of the lungs, dysentery and hookworm anemia.
- A twenty-five-year-old man with congestive heart failure, secondary to rheumatic heart disease.
- A child with kwashiorkor (protein-calorie malnutrition).
- A man needing below-knee amputation for gangrene of the foot.
- A child with massive infection of the foot, secondary to a puncture wound from a thorn.
- A five-year-old boy with abdominal TB and hookworm anemia.
- A sixty-seven-year-old woman with leprosy.

She spent extra time with her leprosy patients because no one had a tougher life in Nepal than its estimated 150,000 leprosy sufferers. Before the 1960s, people with this chronic disease were treated like criminals. They were confined in two small village enclaves and denied any treatment. Their society first banished them and then stripped them of any inheritance they might have claimed. Understandably, people did everything they could to hide their leprosy.

Pressured by the World Health Organization, the government of Nepal finally repealed the country's archaic laws and consented to having leprosy patients treated in their homes. Those with complications would be hospitalized.

Inhumane legal barriers may have disappeared, but the social stigma of leprosy remained. Doctors tried to soften the harshness of the diagnosis by calling it Hansen's disease (named after the man who isolated the bacteria) but "leprosy" stuck.

Helen had a special heart for these people who were made to suffer terrible indignities, as if their physical suffering was not enough. She learned all she could about the disease from medical courses, discovering in the process why there was a need for specialists known as leprologists—the disease is so extremely complex it warrants specialists of its own.

Some of Helen's Hindu friends and colleagues had little sympathy for improving the lot of leprosy patients. They believed such patients were merely getting what they deserved for the sins of a past life. And many of the patients considered themselves vile and contemptible, with no hope in this life or the next.

Helen's leprosy treatment was sometimes a creative mix of medicine and mothering, tailored to the circumstances. A middle-aged lady with a huge ulcerating wound on her knee came to be examined at the hospital. She had been ejected by her family and forced to live alone in a hayloft. At night rats crawled through the hay and gnawed at the wound on her knee; she kept on sleeping because her leg had no feeling.

For two months Helen treated her at Amp Pipal and then prepared to send her home with the ulcer almost healed. Both hands extended, Nepali-style, the doctor gave her patient a packet of pills. But she knew that medication in itself was incomplete treatment. She then placed in her arms a healthy cat to take home, a hunter to keep the rats under control.

By 1979 more than 300 patients with leprosy were attending Amp Pipal as outpatients. A separate building was added to the hospital, now becoming a complex of buildings, for the care of TB and leprosy patients. The New Life Centre was appropriately named, for these patients literally felt that they could begin to live again after a walking death.

Buddhiman Bahadur, 42 years old, had lost several fingers and toes and had crippled hands as a result of leprosy. The disease had so damaged the sensory nerves to his feet that he had lost all feeling. He was able to walk, but a wound on his sole had developed into a large ulcer that would not heal. He had also lost the power to close his eyelids and unless he received a tendon transplant operation, his cornea would dry out and he would go blind.

Buddhi had been totally rejected by his village and his family. He lived alone in a small hut at the edge of a forest and no one dared to come near him. Although his crippled unfeeling hands could scarcely cope, he struggled to cook for himself.

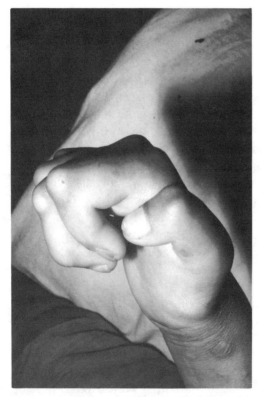
Leprosy patient with "claw hand" deformity.

Yet when this man came to see Dr. Helen he managed to smile. He had heard about Jesus, the one who cured leprosy patients and the one who still loved and offered hope even to them, the most despised of all people.

After exchanging a few words with Buddhiman Bahadur in the outpatient clinic, Helen asked him into her office and closed the door to shut out the noise. They talked together, doctor and patient, and then she picked up her Bible and read the twenty-third Psalm. . . . "Though I walk through the valley of the shadow of death, I will fear no evil for thou art with me."

She got as far as the last line, "Surely goodness and mercy shall follow me all the days of my life . . ." but could not go on. The lump in her throat was just too much.

Buddhiman Bahadur finished it for her: ". . . and I shall dwell in the house of the Lord forever."

37

The Book Burning— A New Fire Kindled

Nationwide strife and uprisings that began in 1979 carried on into the early eighties and spread into the mountains. Trouble had been slowly brewing in Nepal. Corruption and social injustice pushed the country to the brink of widespread protests and violent riots. Even in peaceful Amp Pipal, young people were drawn into hostilities.

So much had changed so quickly. In early mission days, students had been keen to learn, respectful of authority and grateful to have teachers who so genuinely cared about their futures. Now there were grumblings that the mission was a Western plot to take advantage of the people and make money from the villagers.

Helen was away when the anger in Amp Pipal came to a head. Perhaps she would have been able to placate the students when the

186

rebellious national mood hit the schools. It might also have made a difference if the UMN had still been allowed an active role in the school it had started in 1958. But the Department of Education had taken over the schools in 1973, and mission teachers who had been fluent in the language and capable of holding the students' respect were no longer allowed to teach.

The first signs of trouble were just skirmishes. In one class at Amp Pipal, teenage boys threatened to beat up their teacher. Later, a mob of noisy schoolchildren marched down the hill to the teashops near the hospital and demanded, again with threats of violence, that the owners lower their prices. Gangs of kids fought openly in Lapsibot school.

Political agitation, incited primarily by young communists, and anti-Christian feeling reached a peak in August, 1982. After news reached the village that the staff of the UMN hospital in Tansen were on strike, Amp Pipal Hospital felt the strain of staff unrest. A handful of agitators kept feelings of animosity between the UMN and the Nepali staff stirred up.

Rumours and whisperings turned into real trouble the day of Gaiyatra Festival on August 4, celebrated to honour the cow. It was a Gaiyatra tradition for people to post messages, political or otherwise, on the outside of houses and buildings.

Dr. Margaretta Hook, the doctor from Sweden who had succeeded Tom Hale as medical director, at first planned to ignore the cartoons and scrawled messages posted on the inner walls of the hospital, although they depicted missionaries and Christianity crudely. She changed her mind when the staff gathered for morning tea and she saw a poster which ridiculed the figure of Jesus. Shortly before noon she arranged for all the posters on hospital walls to be taken down.

Several hours later she opened her office door in response to a knock and confronted five hostile young men from her hospital staff. A cashier acted as spokesman. "Who removed the posters?" he demanded.

When Dr. Hook refused to give names and informed the men that posters were not to be placed inside any buildings, they stomped off in anger. When she arrived at the hospital the following morning, she noticed that plaques of Nepali scripture verses had been ripped from the walls and thrown on the floor.

Later, as she performed the morning's surgery in the operating room, an angry mob of students streamed down the path from the school and converged on the hospital and began to throw rocks on the roof. Then they pushed their way inside and demanded to see the medical director. "Who took the posters down?" they shouted.

"How is it that you know about the posters?" asked the gentle but no-nonsense nursing superintendent, Klara Petersen. She had a strong hunch that a certain member of the hospital staff had incited this riot, and could truthfully answer that she didn't know anything about the posters.

They surrounded Britt Johansson, a Swedish Community Health worker and threatened to beat her up. One aggressive young fellow tried to twist her arm. Britt, a strong and substantial person herself, refused to retaliate. "Do what you want," she said, "I won't be the first Christian to have suffered."

The seething mob of students then turned around and charged into the hospital building, toward the leprosy examining room that doubled as a chapel.

Grabbing every book they could lay their hands on, they tore back outside and threw armloads of books onto a bonfire one of them had started beside the *chautara*. Cheering and jeering, they danced triumphantly as the fire destroyed Bibles, hymnbooks, patient files, medical journals and health pamphlets.

When Margaretta emerged from the O.R., the angry students had disappeared. She walked to the *maidan*, still wearing her operating clothes. A breeze from the mountains blew grey smoke through the branches of the great pipal tree.

She hung her head, watching the still-glowing embers and thought about the dark days of Germany in the 1930s when the Nazis destroyed "subversive" books.

From the shadowy hillside above the hospital, someone else watched from a distance. The hospital's head cashier, Purna Lal, stayed out of sight.

As news of the book burning flashed through the community's word-of-mouth hotline, adults of the village were shocked that the hospital staff had been treated as enemies. In their twenty-four years of work at Amp Pipal, they felt the mission people had only contributed to the community and they considered them friends.

Purna Lal and other known communist agitators had definitely been behind the attack and should be fired from the staff, advised Shambu

Lal, the same respected elder who had officiated years earlier at the land transfer.

The day after the riot, Shambu Lal appeared at the hospital with four police officers, but this time his advice was radically different. Purna Lal should not be fired, he said, but should simply be given a warning. Something had clearly been going on behind the scenes; what influence had been exerted during the night?

Then Shambu Lal asked to address the entire staff. He told them clearly that the hospital had every right to put up Christian messages and to have hymnbooks and Bibles because the building was a Christian temple. Hindus regarded all religions as holy, he reminded them, and sacred books of any religion were to be treated with respect.

The incident was over but could not be forgotten by the mission workers. They appreciated the goodwill of the political leaders and most of the villagers but remained wary. Purna Lal had not been dislodged from either his job as hospital cashier or his position of influence over the staff.

*****

The fire had burned itself out and all that remained of the health pamphlets and Bibles was a pile of smouldering ashes. But in one young man's heart, a new kind of fire had just begun to burn.

A strong and handsome senior student at Amp Pipal school, Ram Chandra was also bright and articulate. His high-caste Brahmin family was relatively well-off. He seemed like the perfect candidate to be groomed as a communist youth leader and he willingly conformed to the role.

Ram Chandra had been one of the leaders of the student riot and had helped throw papers and Bibles on the fire beside the hospital. But watching the flames consume the curling pages, he suddenly lost his desire to celebrate with his friends. It felt like a hollow victory.

Almost ten years after the incident, he describes the way he felt as the fire raged on.

"I was so puzzled at the people from the hospital. They could see how angry and out of control we were, but they weren't afraid and they weren't angry. I couldn't believe that some were actually praying for us as we burned their Bibles.

189

"After leaving high school I started a good job at a travel agency in Kathmandu. But I had no peace. I was still a communist leader but a few times I attended a Christian church to see what was going on. I wondered if what they taught could possibly be true. I began to read a Nepali Bible.

"One day I read from John's gospel: 'There is no fear in love, but perfect love casts out fear.'

"I decided to put all my trust in Jesus. He gave me an incredible peace that cannot be found anywhere else.

"Later I studied at a Bible school in India and now I am back with my own people as their pastor.

"What is my dream now? That every home in my country receives the same message that set me free."

*****

On a Saturday morning in December, 1991 Ram Chandra stood at the front of the open-raftered church in Amp Pipal, wearing slightly tattered pants and an old black suit jacket. Seating on *gundris* (rice-straw mats) and interspersed among the Nepali believers, Christians from several foreign countries listened to him teach from the Bible using illustrations from life in the mountains:

"When we get to the Marsyandi River, we take the suspension bridge across to Turturi. There is no other way to cross.

"Jesus is the bridge to life and the bridge to heaven."

In the hills and mountains of Nepal where everyone must walk to survive and where footpaths are essential, Ram Chandra told his listeners, "Jesus is the way. He will show us the right path, and help us to walk in it."

38

Power, Perversion and Prayer

In the middle of May, 1984, Alison and I received a note written on the back of an old Christmas card. *"Swagatam"* was written at the top in bold letters. The Nepali word for "welcome" had clustered around it little musical notes and cheery words like laughter, strength, peace, joy. On the bottom, after "Delighted you're coming to be boss and pal!," it was signed by Helen.

We looked forward to seeing Helen again. We had already been with the UMN for ten years and I had been requested to go to Amp Pipal as acting medical director for a four-month term, between the departure of one director and the arrival of another.

One week after arriving in the beautiful village, I could see we were in trouble. The medical director I was to replace, Dr. Margaretta Hook, had been trying valiantly to keep the lid on simmering staff unrest. I re-oriented myself, hardly believing this was the Amp Pipal Hospital

I had known. A few days before her departure (my arrival overlapped a bit with the end of her term), an angry delegation from the staff surrounded Margaretta, demanding to know why another member of the staff had not yet received sick leave pay.

Her calmly delivered reply must have incensed the leaders, because they immediately summoned other staff from their work to join them. They wanted a better answer, they insisted, or they would all walk off their jobs.

The leader and spokesman was a slender, handsome fellow in a lightweight pale blue safari suit. His manner appeared outwardly civil and courteous, and although he smiled as he spoke, his words had a cutting edge to them. I was told he was the elected representative of the entire staff, and the hospital's head cashier.

It dawned on me suddenly—this was Purna Lal, the local boy who had grown up to wield such influence over the youth and leaders of the community. I looked at him with curiosity. How had he acquired such polish and sophistication? Was this the same communist activist who had incited the village schoolboys to rioting and book burning?

Margaretta succeeded in placating the agitators and they returned to their jobs and told everyone else to do likewise. But we all wondered what was coming next.

Three weeks into my term my suspicions of impending trouble were proven right. I remember the day, it was on Thursday, July 19, that our hospital's business manager, Winnie Lau, pinned a notice on the wall of the staff tea-room. It announced a five per cent increase in salaries for all staff.

A raise was hardly the stuff for creating a furor, but Purna Lal and his ringleaders were primed to pounce. This increase, they raged, was nothing less than insulting and disgraceful. It would not be tolerated. Someone must go to UMN headquarters in Kathmandu immediately to protest—and of course, that someone should be the staff representative, Purna Lal.

As the new medical director, I told the staff that I could not agree with their method of protest. I explained that Purna Lal was our only qualified cashier (his associate was on leave) and he could not be spared. I gave him a direct order to stay at work.

The staff leaders then walked off and the next report that came to me was that Purna Lal had not only left for Kathmandu, but had taken another hospital employee with him. What he told the staff before leaving I'll never know, but nurses and cleaners and office staff proceeded to walk off their jobs. Everyone strolled up to the *chautara* above the hospital, and there they sat sombrely under the big pipal tree.

Shobha, our newly appointed Nepali nursing superintendent, drew up a roster for ward duty the first night of the strike, calling on every available source of help. The missionary families pitched in to meet the most urgent needs, although they could never hope to do the work of 65 employees.

Before leaving the hospital on the first night of the strike, I made arrangements to send a runner to notify Shambu Lal and the Chief District Officer in Gorkha of the possibility of violence or vandalism, and a second runner to get help from the police at Tadhi Pokhari. Then I tried to get some rest, but a fever and hacking cough, piled on top of the problems that were my responsibility to solve, allowed little sleep. In my journal for July 19, 1984, I recorded:

"Sore throat, cough and malaise. None of us are in despair, although we fear for the really ill patients. Here is where we need to trust in the Everlasting Arms, not only to guide us but to keep away all bitterness and recrimination."

Strike or no strike, Helen always got up early, and at 5:30 the next morning she was at my door with a letter she had prepared to be run to the Chief District Officer. She took a good look at me, heard my cough and told me to go back to bed. If the staff wanted to meet with the medical director, she would take my place.

At mid-morning I staggered out of bed to answer the party line phone. Helen's voice sounded strained. "Gerry, I've got some good news, and some that's not so good," she said. "The staff will return to work, but they're insisting on one condition."

I waited. "Purna Lal must not be punished for going to Kathmandu against your orders."

I shook myself fully awake. "That's impossible!" I almost shouted into the phone. "He should be fired! If we give in he'll have not only the staff but the administration under his thumb. Who knows what he'll do next?"

Helen fully agreed with me, but she didn't think the strike would end unless we accepted their terms. "Think about it," she said. "They've prepared a statement for you to sign. I'll bring it up for you to read."

I crawled back into bed, feeling like the condemned man who has to choose which way to die.

As I waited for Helen I weighed the case. Maybe the welfare of the sick patients was the most important factor. I was aware that settling a strike quickly, before the two sides get dug in, is a wise strategy.

Helen arrived with the statement and I signed it. I felt I had made a concession to evil to bring about a good result. The staff immediately returned to work, and the following day Purna Lal and his friend arrived back from Kathmandu and resumed their duties.

The whole experience was humbling and chastening for me. I had conceded the battle to these smiling deceptive men who loved to stir up trouble. There would be other battles, and I hadn't yet admitted defeat.

A good housecleaning was much needed, beginning with Purna Lal, but it would be a tricky business. I had signed a statement that he would not be punished; any action against him would certainly ignite another strike. Two of his colleagues needed to be dismissed too, but that action could follow later.

The situation was absolutely intolerable, but none of us missionaries could see any way out. Each one realized that our only hope lay in seeking daily guidance from the Lord. We just had to admit defeat and throw ourselves onto His mercy.

Before leaving Amp Pipal, Margaretta had received a letter from a company in India, Peejay Industries, asking her to verify the medical expenses of one of their employees. His wife was reported to have had an operation in Amp Pipal Hospital earlier in the year and he had submitted a large claim to the company. The employee had already been reimbursed, but the company now wanted details and confirmation of the wife's treatment.

In our hand we had the company's copy of an itemized statement with an illegible signature of someone in our cashier's office. We searched our files and could find no record of the operation or the patient. The village given as the employee's address did not exist.

Now we had strong evidence that the claim was fictitious. Could there have been collusion between the Peejay employee and someone in our hospital's discharge office so that the employee could claim a large sum of money from his company?

Head cashier Purna Lal was asked to help, but he claimed to know nothing about the statement and said he couldn't assist in deciphering the signature.

Through letters that travelled back and forth between Amp Pipal and Peejay Industries, we learned that the employee had confessed the claim to be false and had returned the money. The company then sent us a photocopy of a note, signed by one of our health assistants, in support of the false claim.

This signature was legible. I called Nagendra into my office and showed him the note bearing his signature. He turned pale and sat in silence in front of me for several minutes, his head down and his eyes averted. He admitted that he had written and signed the letter of support, but would say nothing more.

I decided to deal later with Nagendra's part in this apparent deceit. I was more concerned with finding the originator of the fraudulent claim. Not a single letter of the signature could be identified. But it had one interesting feature, under the name was a broad, sweeping horizontal stroke with two little dots at the end.

We needed more clues. We browsed through a couple of receipt books. The signature of one cashier, Mohan, bore no resemblance to the forged name. But on page after page of receipts, we came across another signature with a feature that riveted our attention. The name with two dots under a horizontal stroke was none other than Purna Lal's!

My heart literally skipped a beat! Then it raced like fury as I suddenly realized the real significance of this startling piece of evidence.

It seemed irrefutable: Purna Lal had made up the false claim and forged the signature.

Now we could perhaps start the "housecleaning."

But first, we needed help and advice on how to proceed. We contacted UMN headquarters and Howard Barclay, now Executive Secretary of the UMN, agreed to leave his workload behind and come out to Amp Pipal. He told us he had already sought legal advice in Kathmandu, and he impressed upon me the necessity of dismissing Purna Lal. But if we mishandled the case, another strike would be inevitable.

If some of us grieved over a deplorable situation, Helen grieved more. It was an agonizing time for her. The "Hospital of the Living Word" had degenerated into a hotbed of evil. A small group of political perverts had somehow taken over and now had the whole hospital operation at their mercy.

After the strike the missionaries from the hospital and Community Health met at frequent Team meetings. Everyone was kept informed of the situation. We prayed often. Nor did we leave out Purna Lal in our prayers. This man needed our compassion, not our condemnation.

But he also needed to be fired. We pulled together all our documentary evidence and set August 14 as the dismissal day, although I was still at a loss about the exact course of action to take. The evening before D-Day, with every single member of our UMN team in attendance, Helen prayed for guidance about how to handle Purna Lal. During her prayer I had a sudden flash of insight and knew, beyond a shadow of a doubt, how to handle tomorrow.

Purna Lal must be fired, no doubt about that, but first of all Nagendra must be summoned to the office early in the day and handed a stern written warning of complicity in an obvious fraud. Later, Purna Lal would be dismissed for the same reason, his punishment being more severe because of numerous past misdemeanours.

Purna Lal would be given the opportunity to resign, with no questions asked, or he could object to the charges and ask that the UMN conduct an official enquiry into his case.

First thing the next morning I called Nagendra back into the office and handed him a strongly-worded warning for his part in writing a false letter of support. Any further misconduct of any kind would mean dismissal. He offered no objection.

I told Purna Lal to come to my office at 5:30 p.m. and asked Shobha, the nursing superintendent, to stay in the office with me. Purna Lal appeared on schedule, looking relaxed and confident in his pale blue safari suit.

I began by reminding him in general terms of the trouble he had caused the hospital. Not a feather was ruffled. "I've done nothing wrong," he said, leaning back in his chair. "I work hard and you'll never find me guilty of doing anything bad."

I got down to more specifics. He looked me boldly in the eye, unimpressed, and answered each charge with cool detachment, his voice smooth and even in tone. "I know nothing about your burning books. The staff voted to strike because of the miserable salary increase. I went to Kathmandu because they asked me to go as their representative. And I have no idea what you mean by threats and bullying."

I looked at his hand resting casually on the corner of my desk, exchanged glances with Shobha and took a deep breath. The time had come for hard evidence.

I produced the false claim and laid it carefully beside 35 copies of his ordinary signature. I pointed out the general similarity and then finally, drew specific attention to the tell-tale two dots under the broad horizontal stroke.

He suddenly changed. His lips tightened and turned pale. His hand on the corner of my desk began to shake and then fell away. He glanced furtively toward the door and, as if realizing there was no escape, slumped in his chair.

I told him he was being charged with fraud, a serious crime. If he chose to claim innocence, his case would be subjected to an inquiry. If he resigned, no charges would be laid and no further action would be taken.

For a fleeting moment Purna Lal didn't move a muscle. Then in an instant he lost his polished coolness. Like a trapped rattler with fangs bared, he lashed out with a tirade in his own language. Most of this Nepali was mercifully beyond my understanding, but Shobha told me later that nothing and no one had escaped his wrath.

"What is your choice, Purna Lal?" I asked after he had calmed down.

He would resign, he spat at me. I passed him a pen and a sheet of paper. He grabbed the pen in his clenched fist and pushed it across the paper, stabbing in furor at the end of every sentence.

"I hereby resign . . ." and then, at the end of the page, he signed his name, completing it from force of habit with a horizontal stroke and underneath, two small dots.

The three of us walked together to the office for his last paycheque. Winnie Lau, our diminutive office manager from Hong Kong, spoke gently to Purna Lal. "I have prayed for you often," she said, "and I will keep on praying."

Something about Winnie's words, or how she said them, had a calming effect on Purna Lal and he regained some of his poise. He shook each of our hands, Western-style, and actually thanked us. We could only hope this hard experience might alter the course of the life of this gifted man.

At the end of September, Alison and I walked out of Amp Pipal after what we considered the most traumatic and worrisome period of our lives. Our respect for and friendship with Helen had deepened during these four months. Her overall understanding of the Nepali culture, her rapport with all members of the staff, and her wisdom and patience had been priceless contributions to a successful outcome.

I doubt we could have achieved much without Helen in the role of reconciler and forgiver. She constantly spoke up for the good qualities in Purna Lal—an effective counterweight to the wrongs and evils that the rest of us were constantly talking about.

And when the stress level got high, Helen would invite us up for dinner. In some miraculous way she always seemed to find some special, tasty treat for her guests, probably saved up for the occasion. The good food, laughter and warm fellowship did wonders.

I wondered at Helen's unshakeable optimism when the integrity of the hospital seemed to be falling apart before our eyes. Her enduring faith in God enabled her to hold her head high when there was every reason for gloom and despair.

39

Hospitality and Hilarity

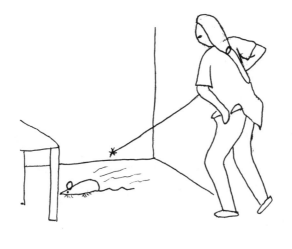

On the evening of Wednesday, December 28, 1988 Alison and I dined with Helen in her little thatched house.

In one corner of the area set aside for eating we sat on padded mats resting on a *gundri* which, in turn, rested on the mud floor. In front of us a long, low table displayed utensils, plates and eatables. When she wasn't running to and from the kitchen, Helen perched herself on a low stool across the table from us. Tata had gone home for the day.

Before leaving, she had prepared food for the guests: a tasty thick potato-onion soup, cauliflower with cheese sauce followed up by her celebrated lemon pudding. She and Helen had concocted for us the Amp Pipal equivalent of a seven-course banquet.

Not surprisingly, we were not the only guests sitting around the low-slung table. At one end sat two people from the village of Gaikhur, a young man and a boy. The man, who suffered from weakness and wasting of both legs from old polio, walked slowly and shakily. The left arm of the nine-year-old boy showed marked deformity from a badly healed fracture of the elbow.

They sat there quietly and said little but seemed to enjoy the unaccustomed food. They had come from their village to attend the regular Wednesday evening prayer meeting in Amp Pipal.

As usual, dining with Helen proved to be a pleasant experience, but it was not without its interruptions. Three times we heard gentle-but-audible knocks at the door; for each Helen got up to welcome the visitor. Why had they come? To enquire about a relative in the hospital; to sell firewood or eggs; to find out the location of the prayer meeting. In each case they received from Helen a smile and an answer that seemed to satisfy them.

Helen's home was a typical Nepali house with mud floors (consisting of a mixture of special clay, cow dung and water), and boasted what Helen called "the luxury of running water and light." Unfortunately, you couldn't drink the water and the electricity often failed. She wanted the simple life and these two amenities made it tolerable.

The lights allowed her to read in the evenings and to scribble away at her correspondence. Running water enabled her to have a "pour bath" every now and then. Standing in a plastic basin discreetly concealed in a curtained-off corner of her kitchen, she could soap up and then pour water to her heart's content. "Fabulous," she called it, "Better than a shower."

The little thatched house had other fine features, including a front *piri* (verandah) that commanded a spectacular view of the broad Chepi river valley and the white Annapurna mountains beyond. A precarious staircase led to Helen's upstairs bedroom and storage area. Few people were permitted to inspect the latter! Overnight guests could sleep on the outside verandah upstairs, also a vantage point for glorious views of the snowy peaks.

Helen had to admit there were some not-so-good things. No one had figured out a way to keep bugs and rats out of the thatched roof. Many times she had to scare off crows pecking off bits of thatch to get at the bugs. Invariably the thatch would begin leaking after a year or two, necessitating a large plastic sheet over her bed. As the sheet filled up, she would direct it to empty into a bucket in what she called "controlled leaking."

Many women show little affection for spiders and salamanders but for Helen they were friends—allies in the battle to control invading bugs. When Gary and Dorothy Gibson from Camrose, Alberta visited Helen in 1984, they commented on "the rats, the lack of a fridge and the little smoky kerosene cooking stove."

"How could she live with caterpillars, rats, shrews, fleas and bed-bugs?" they asked.

But for the Gibsons, the ultimate in hardship and discomfort was Helen's outdoor *charpi* (toilet). The Asian "squat" type, it was reachable only by walking outside to the back and climbing up thirteen steep stone steps. Once the UMN offered to build a proper indoor toilet but she declined.

If this little Nepali house was a place of prayer and meditation, even more was it a house of hospitality. Countless people from all castes and villages had been welcomed to come in and sit down on the covered trunk by the door. Many then made their way to the long coffee table where Helen shared her food with them.

An equally warm and sincere welcome awaited visitors from across the seas. Michael Bracko, a thirty-two-year-old student from a university in Utah, visited Amp Pipal for one week in December, 1986 after trekking in the Mt. Everest area. A couple of years later he wrote some of his impressions:

". . . Helen didn't know me very well but she welcomed me into her home. . . .

"Helen would always listen to what you were saying. . . . This was very evident when she was talking to Nepalis. She would look them right in the eye and listen to every word they said. I was touched by her love for the people of Nepal.

"Her influence made me a better person. . . . I have become a more pleasant person, less materialistic, and closer to God."

Dr. Mark Zimmerman from New York spent two years in Nepal with the UMN, including most of 1986 at Amp Pipal. During that time he wrote a daily journal, bits of which are excerpted:

"I had dinner tonight with Helen Huston. She is a doctor in her late 50s who pioneered the project here at Amp Pipal. . . . She has been here since

1960 and has seen a small dispensary grow into a hospital, and a community health program grow where there was none.

". . . She gestures with large, skillful hands and fixes one with a sharp gaze when she talks of her love for medicine.

(After he became ill) *". . . she wanted to know if there was anything that she could make me that I might feel like eating. She really was serious and sincere about the 'anything.' Later she sent packages of Kool-Aid, instant soup, bread, and stewed fruit. I am sure she must have put a sizeable dent in her supply of these packaged things.*

". . . It feels reassuring to have someone in your corner who you know cares."

* * * * *

A monumental banging and clatter woke Sheila Findlay from a sound sleep. A UMN colleague, she was staying at Helen's home overnight, in the quiet and peaceful village of Amp Pipal.

Loud crashing noises jarred her awake instantly. She reached for the flashlight beside her, tiptoed to the bedroom door and shone a light into the dark livingroom.

There she saw a moving spectre, its right hand brandishing a poker high in the air and its left clasping loose fitting pyjama bottoms that had seen better days.

Helen was in hot pursuit of a rat. The sight alone should have been enough to scare any rat. The poor rodent scampered in and out behind cupboards and chairs, over cushions and around table legs, in a frantic effort to elude its pursuer.

Sheila wondered who to cheer for: the rat hunter who was quick with her poker, but not quite quick enough, or the rat who invariably scampered to a new spot just a split second ahead of the crashing poker.

The racket was unbelievable. Sheila wondered if it disturbed patients in the hospital 185 metres away. At last there was a final mighty whack, followed by a loud "Hooray" from Helen. Helen had got the better of the rat and one rat down was worth a celebration.

To this day, Sheila cannot recall ever seeing anything quite as comical as Helen's one-armed poker-flailing pyjama-holding battle against a single hapless rodent.

Helen draws enjoyment out of life. It's not that she is constantly telling jokes so much as it is her ability to see the funny, the ridiculous and the absurd going on around her, especially in herself. Mark Zimmerman talked about ". . . the hilarious atmosphere generated by her laughter. First her body shook with laughter, then the room, then you had no choice but be caught up in it."

She won't ever laugh at the mistake of someone else, but the ability to laugh at her own mistakes got her through all kinds of tough circumstances, like it did the day she rushed to finish her clinic to be on time, for once, for dinner at Tom and Cynthia Hales. This would be an interesting evening, dining with the Chief District Officer of the Gorkha District who was paying his first visit to Amp Pipal Hospital.

In accordance with one of Murphy's Laws, the workload is usually heaviest on the day you want to get away on time. No matter how hard Helen worked to meet the needs and requests of the out-patients, the line stayed long. For two consecutive patients, both young women, she ordered chest X-rays, and between seeing other patients, she called back the first of the two.

"I'm sorry, my dear," she told the young woman, as she showed her the X-ray in the viewing box. "It appears that you have TB. That left lung looks like a pretty advanced case."

The young woman looked quizzically at Helen. "Are you sure about this, doctor?" she asked. "The pain I'm having is all on my right side."

The girl was right. Helen re-checked the names and discovered that the films had somehow been reversed and she was looking at the X-rays of the second patient.

She apologized profusely to the girl, who accepted the revised news graciously, much relieved that her own X-ray showed lungs which were free of the disease.

By the time Helen finished her last patient, rushed out of the hospital and climbed the hundred or so steps up to Hale's house, she was out breath. Tom welcomed her in and ushered her to dinner which was already in progress. She greeted the CDO whom she had met earlier in the day; he got up from his rice meal to say *"Namaste."*

Then Tom introduced her to their second guest, a young lady. The face looked familiar—a second later, too familiar. Was it really the girl whose X-rays she had muddled with someone else's? No doubt about it, it was her.

There was no need to apologize about it this time. Both of them just threw back their heads and laughed and laughed. Who was this girl anyway? The CDO was her uncle and when she quickly told him about the wrong-sided X-rays, he thought is was a great joke too.

Helen's ability to laugh at herself and her own mistake did wonders to build a warm bridge of friendship with the CDO's office in Gorkha.

*****

The doctors who had been involved in Helen's surgery at Patan Hospital in Kathmandu in July, 1983, knew that not everyone would appreciate the Valentine they had in mind, but they calculated that Helen would. And they were right, for she could boast that "Nobody else has a Valentine like mine!"

The conspiring doctors designed their creation around an unusual picture taken of her, trimmed a heart-shaped border, mounted it on heavy white paper and had a visiting artist, Rev. Ted Davey from Toronto, decorate it with an ornate curlicued and frilled border. It resembled a real work of art—if held at a distance.

Helen's Norwegian friends, Asbjorn and Mia Voreland, were guests at her home in Amp Pipal the night the Valentine arrived in the mail. After saying good night, Helen began to open some of her mail. First the Vorelands heard a few chuckles from her bedroom, then a sudden escalation into gales of laughter. They crept out of their bed on the verandah and went to look at the Valentine in her hand. There, in living color, was a sharp, clear picture of Helen's "insides" taken during her operation the summer before. It wasn't the sort of thing one would hang in a living room, but nevertheless not a bad picture, and definitely one worth framing.

"My dear surgical colleagues," Helen wrote by way of thanks for their thoughtfulness, "I feel deeply honoured to receive a Valentine from you. I had the privilege of opening it by candlelight in my bedroom last night. Two notable guests (Norwegian) were sleeping on my upstairs verandah at the time. The Valentine threw me, and them, into convulsions. I showed it to the surgeon here but he said it didn't look like me. I am deeply indebted to those who opened me up. Thanks, pals."

40

Sparkling Pages
and Tough Decisions

Every few years, Helen made the same resolution. She would catch up on her neglected correspondence, and never let it drown her again.

It seemed like a worthy objective. But in her case, it was completely unattainable.

Try as she might to pare it down to size, the mound of unanswered letters continued to grow as if fed from some mysterious underground source.

She grew accustomed to the size of it, and much like the people who put signs on their overloaded office desks saying, "This is my desk and I like it this way," Helen could normally ignore the rising stack of paper.

But during a forced rest, such as an illness, the pile screamed for her attention. Problem was, she received mail constantly. At one stage, her mailing list comprised more than 900 names, somewhat more than the United Church's limit of 150 for each missionary. It meant she had to rely on friends to help run off copies of her twice yearly prayer letters and to mail them to the excess 750 friends.

She tried to be a faithful letter writer. For 36 years, she wrote weekly to her parents, and after the death of her father, corresponded on a near-weekly basis with her Vancouver friend Mildred Sullivan.

She wrote some letters by candlelight, starting at 4:00 a.m. and staying solidly at her task until the mail runner left at 7:00; others while sitting in Nepali teashops; more as she travelled on planes. She wrote thousands of them.

She never wrote a dull or a flat letter. The pages sparkled with graphic descriptions, amusing anecdotes and heart-rending tales.

Her Norwegian friend Mia Voreland called her a fantastic writer. "Getting a letter from her is such a joy. You can almost hear her voice through it. And she usually scribbles all over the place!"

Scribble she did—on margins, flaps, the backs of envelopes, words like "love galore," "much joy to you," "fun and blessings." It was hard to find any wasted white space.

Sometimes a letter from Helen would be written on an old Christmas card or on the back of an out-of-date newsletter. It didn't really matter what kind of writing paper she used—the words were bound to turn into laughter, or sometimes tears, at the other end.

Most of her individual and all of the circular letters contained words of prayer and praise and expressions of gratitude. In one letter she asked for prayer for someone whose husband had just taken his own life, for a young man training to be a leprosy paramedical worker, for young Nepalis working in the Butwal Technical Institute. In the same letter she expressed thanks for those who prayed "and got me through the Convocation address in Edmonton."

When she made these frequent resolutions to get her correspondence under control, she struggled desperately to thank each person or group that had made a contribution toward the work at Amp Pipal.

But she could hardly make a dent, much less catch up.

Her friend, Dr. Eleanor Knox from Australia, accepted Helen's mountain of correspondence as "a feature of her life." Wherever she goes, she said, "she takes it with her and she brings it back again, not much reduced, more having been added in the meantime."

It was easy to tell when the mountain was completely out of control. Her letters would then begin, "Alas, I can't seem to find your latest letter," or "Thank you so much for your letter which seems to have gotten misplaced."

She finally hit upon a brilliantly devised system. She started two piles of letters; one marked "Urgent" and the other "Must answer."

It didn't make much of a contribution to the solution, but she felt better about the way the original pile had shrunk to half its size. Two small Lig Ligs looked more manageable than one Mt. Everest.

*****

At a retreat held in Pokhara in 1988, the ten UMNers who were members of the United Church of Canada heard some disturbing reports from home.

The principal of a United Church college in Canada had stated, in a panel discussion on the topic of theological diversity, that he was doing everything he could to remove Jesus Christ from the centre of the Church's theology so that the church could "move forward into the modern era."

Another report stated in Montreal that the pastoral care minister at United Theological College had married another man in a homosexual wedding in the United Church.

Helen had long since learned to be accepting and forgiving of people. She probably inherited the genes of tolerance and understanding from her father's acceptance of other people. And her mother had brought her up with the teaching to "always make excuses for the behaviour of others. There's no telling but the other one might have a headache or have had bad news that day."

Helen had learned to not judge other Christians whose lives might be full of doubts and inconsistencies. After all, she was a pretty superficial believer herself when her ship docked at Bombay in 1953. Not that she didn't have some pretty strong and carefully thought out opinions on important issues. Her view, backed up with Scripture, was that homosexuals should be welcomed into the fellowship of the church in the same way as the greedy businessman or the couple with a drinking problem. Every single person in the church is in need of forgiveness and reconciliation with God. But, she believed, if they are unwilling to repent and give up wrongdoing, they should not be allowed to minister in the name of Jesus.

She found it utterly astonishing that suggestions coming out of the United Church were that Islam, Buddhism, Hinduism and Christianity were all paths leading to the same God. She had seen the difference all too closely. She loved her Hindu friends and patients, but it broke her heart to see women going out and bowing down to a rock in the middle of the roadway. She had seen the Hindu caste system that treated some people like dogs, the degradation of women who cannot bear sons, the fear and terror engendered by evil spirits and angry gods.

For 36 years the United Church of Canada had supported her work, but now she prayed for a way out that would honour God and at the same time not hurt or offend the people she loved.

It was again her furlough time in Canada, and after deep soul-searching she submitted her resignation to the Division of World Outreach, the branch of the church responsible for missions. The resignation from the DWO registered her protest without her actually abandoning the church. She wanted to return to Nepal, but where would her support come from now? She decided to leave that problem with "the God who counts the stars and heals the broken-hearted."

News of her resignation quickly spread within the United Church membership. By the time she arrived at the annual meeting of the church's Alberta Conference it was common knowledge.

Stephen Istvanffy, a board member of Southminster United in Calgary, attended the same meeting, and although he had never been introduced to Helen Huston, he knew all about her work in Nepal. During coffee break he introduced himself and before the break was over, got down to brass tacks.

"Would you consider allowing Southminster to support you?" he asked. Seeing the wonder and amazement in her face, he assured her that there was no need to answer right away. It was an offer that touched her deeply, but one sponsoring church would hardly give her enough support. Not a lot was needed to cover her personal needs, but much of the money designated for her work was channeled into the budget of the hospital.

She really needed to be supported by a missionary organization. She was reminded about such an organization, called Interserve, by friends in Vancouver, Doris Bailey and Mildred Sullivan. She had worked alongside many "Interservers"; in fact, a high percentage of the medical personnel in the UMN were connected with this inter-denominational organization that brought together workers from Great Britain, Australia, New Zealand, the United States and Canada, Holland, India, Singapore and Hong Kong.

The Interserve representative in Vancouver, more accustomed to young, inexperienced applicants, encouraged Helen to apply and sent a questionnaire for her to fill out.

"You can't imagine the emptiness I suddenly felt," she says, "when I tried to answer questions like 'Will your church support you?' and 'Is your minister in favour?' All I could think was 'I have no church and no minister.'"

At the same Sylvan Lake Camp where she called out to God in the thunderstorm 43 years earlier, she again felt guided—this time to put aside her misgivings and apply. By the end of June, she had her reply from Bob Morris, the Executive-Director of Canada's Interserve:

"We at Interserve count it a real privilege to welcome Dr. Helen into our fellowship. We know of her faithfulness and fruitfulness as a representative of Jesus Christ in Nepal."

And Southminster United, a church that Will Huston had taken a part in planting years before, met the requirements for a sponsoring church.

On July 2, 1989, the day of her official welcome to Southminster's church family, the members welcomed her as if she had been theirs all along. To conclude the service, they chose one of Helen's favourite hymns, Handel's "Thine be the Glory."

The next month she returned to Nepal, still a member of the United Church of Canada but under the sponsorship of a different mission organization. Picking her way between the rice paddies on the familiar route to the green slopes of Lig Lig Mountain, she caught her first glimpse of the hospital.

"Home!" she shouted.

As she got into her own bed that night, in her own thatch-roofed home, she remembers feeling extremely, unusually happy.

Nothing could touch this happiness, not even the knowledge that this was the beginning of her last term in Nepal.

41

Acclaim and Awards

"Dr. Helen slept here once," said the Nepali hostess who knew just a little English. This sentence she had rehearsed so she could tell it proudly to visitors to her teashop as they passed through the village of Sano Dumri on their way to Amp Pipal.

Her visitor this time was A.C. Forrest, editor of the United Church *Observer*, who had come to Nepal to research a story about Helen Huston's pioneering work in the world's most awesome terrain.

His 1974 front-cover story, entitled "Mission in the Clouds," was the forerunner of many other stories as people from several continents visited Amp Pipal and went home with accounts of her work.

After the monsoon rains in 1979, Canada's largest newspaper, the *Toronto Star*, sent a reporter and a photographer to interview this well-known Canadian missionary doctor. The editors wanted her story to be the first of a four-part "Apostles of Love" series. The second article would be written about the life of Mother Teresa of Calcutta.

Star religion editor Tom Harpur and photographer Bob Olsen slogged their way slowly uphill toward Amp Pipal in the intense afternoon heat. A porter led the way with their gear. They were within sight of the hospital, with six hours behind them and a good hour in front, when they reached a narrow part of the path.

Darkness was beginning to fall when they were hit by near disaster. Tom slipped off the path and was headed for a deep gorge, but his fall was stopped when the straps on his pack caught and became entangled in a bush. Bob heard his frantic cries and, hardly able to see in the darkening twilight, hurried to his friend's rescue, only to fall off the path himself. In the end, their nimble and sturdy sixty-year-old porter rescued them both. Ever so humbly, the two Canadians reached Amp Pipal Hospital and turned right to trudge the last hundred footsteps up to Helen's door.

It was a long way from Yonge Street, but they revived a bit when they received a "Helen welcome," so enthusiastic and friendly it almost made them forget their tiredness.

"Did you enjoy the walk from Dumri?" she asked the beaten men.

"Well, sort of," answered one of them, smiling weakly.

"Is there anything I can get you?"

They brightened. "You wouldn't happen to have a cold beer in the fridge, would you?"

"Sorry," she said, "no beer—and no fridge!" They all laughed.

Tom Harpur and Bob Olsen somehow survived without the cold beer and wrote a well researched article about the Amp Pipal scene.

The special 1979 Christmas edition of the *Toronto Star* "Apostles of Love" article began, "Can the human spirit transcend poverty and despair? It is a question much of the world needs to ask this Christmas. *Star* religion editor Tom Harpur found the answer in India and Nepal—and it is 'yes.'"

A full page and a bit more were devoted to a colourful description of Nepal, the UMN, Amp Pipal and the life and work of Helen Huston.

It is probable that this article revealed more of the heart of Nepal to Canadians than any other publication over the years. The writer was much moved by what he heard and saw at Amp Pipal, and while he had high praise for Helen, he also shared something notable about Will Huston.

"She became very shy," he wrote of Helen, *"when asked about her dedication to sharing herself with the Nepali sick and needy when she could be making a large salary in practice in Canada, but one source of inspiration became obvious. Dr. Huston's eighty-six-year-old father, a retired United Church minister in Alberta, has just written to tell her that he is moving out of his house to a senior citizens' home in order to make room for a newly arrived Vietnamese family. His spirit has clearly borne fruit in her life."*

Tom also wrote about the Amp Pipal Christian community: *"Christmas will be a joyous occasion since all of the staff here experience the spirit of Christmas—giving and sharing—all year long."*

How would Christmas be celebrated in these mountains?

"Rigmor, a fair-haired Norwegian nurse, probably spoke for Helen Huston and the others when she said that on Christmas Eve she will kindle a fire in the hearth, light a few candles, then read over all the mail from family and friends and cry a little, because it's such a special time back home."

Newspapers and magazines in Alberta were among the first to take notice of Helen Huston and her work in faraway Nepal. Her hometown *Rimbey Record* called her a "Latter-day Female Albert Schweitzer," and a *Calgary Herald* feature article was entitled "Alberta Doctor Fighting to Save Lives in Nepal."

At Christmas, 1985, the weekly *Alberta Report's* cover story on "Helping Hands: How Albertans reach out to the Poor Nations," called her work "A Most Saintly Service." Pictures with the article showed Amp Pipal Hospital with the Himalayas as a backdrop and Helen supporting the arm of a little girl with TB.

Helen abhorred the limelight. Compliments and praise made her feel uncomfortable. She constantly kept in mind the biblical warning "Woe to you when all men speak well of you."

And so it was with warm yet uneasy feelings that she read a letter that offered to confer upon her the greatest honour yet. The University of Alberta was inviting her to accept the honorary degree of Doctor of Laws at the Seventy-fifth Annual Convocation on November 16, 1985. In a sense it was a double honour: she had been asked to give the convocation address after receiving the honorary degree.

For months she protested and resisted the idea, finally bowing to the persuasion of friends who made it clear that it is wrong not to "let your light shine before men."

But during the days before the Convocation it looked like she might never make it and would certainly not be ready for it.

The previous weekend Jane Loree had driven her to Lac La Biche, Alberta where Helen was to speak on behalf of missions. After arrival, she fell ill with fever, strep throat and malaise. She improved enough to speak but on Monday relapsed, and slept in the car all the way back to Edmonton.

The next few days were hectic and she could hardly concentrate. She was invited to attend a special meeting of the senate of the university and taken to lunch with Chancellor Robert Savaryn, Mr. Peter Stollery (who also received an honorary degree) and two Nepali students.

Before she realized it, it was the night before the convocation, and she wasn't ready. Too exhausted to prepare her address for the next day, she went to bed early. An hour and a half later she woke up, she recalls, feeling "as sharp as a tack." In a virtual flood of inspiration, she got down on paper all that she wanted to say.

Then it was off in a flurry to the pre-convocation luncheon. She sat between the chancellor and the president, trying to eat, answer hundreds of questions and stay quiet inside at the same time. Before the ceremony she got rapid-fire instructions from the registrar, ran to don cap and gown, had formal pictures taken with the chancellor, and ran again to join the procession entering the Jubilee Auditorium.

She managed to squeeze her brother James' hand as she walked up the aisle and then was conducted to the front row of the platform facing four thousand people. It seemed a long, long way from the villages on the slopes of Lig Lig mountain.

As endurance tests go, she would have preferred the hard day's walk from Tuture to Amp Pipal rather than the three long hours for the conferring of degrees on hundreds of graduates. Each graduate crossed the platform and shook hands with the chancellor. Several of the dignitaries, including Helen, dozed off and on.

She shook herself awake when an honorary degree was bestowed on Mr. Stollery, and then Helen heard herself being introduced.

"... Her commitment to the Nepalese led her to establish the Gorkha Hospital at Amp Pipal where the local inhabitants receive health care otherwise unavailable. Her concern for the welfare of others has distinguished Dr. Huston as a humanitarian and Canadian ambassador of goodwill."

For three hours Helen had been waiting for this moment, but somehow things turned out somewhat differently than she had anticipated. She described it from her perspective.

I had been instructed to stand when Amy [Dr. Amy Zelmer, vice-president of the university] read my name, and to remove my mortarboard so that the registrar could get the thingamabob over my head. As I took it off [the mortarboard], the side combs fell out of my hair. I tried to quickly comb my hair back before four thousand people. Static electricity added to the wild look. Fortunately I was oblivious.

I dropped my hankie. I realized I'd set my mortarboard on Amy's seat and she had to return to it. . . .

Outwardly in a flap, she felt an inner peace as she bowed slightly toward the chancellor and began. "Eminent Chancellor . . ." The chancellor, president, deans of the faculties, graduating students and

Dr. Huston addressing the audience at the convocation.

their families and guests fixed their gaze on the captivating woman wearing the crimson robe and hood of her honorary Doctor of Laws.

Her friend Jane Loree, who sat in the audience that day, later wrote, *"When she began to speak, the auditorium stilled. You could have heard the proverbial pin drop. She looked fresh and her natural enthusiasm came through."*

She said she accepted the honour on behalf of all Canadians who have worked in the "Two-thirds" world or in isolated areas of Canada to bring healing and hope. She spoke of her friends in the hills of Nepal, Bedlia Maya and Iman and Ram Bahadur. She talked about these Nepali friends belonging to the same family as Canadians, "made of the same clay."

And she talked about an illness of the soul. "We are suffering," she said, "from a serious disease, more infectious than AIDS. The disease is pandemic in North America—although I admit it is endemic worldwide. I suffered a relapse myself as soon as I hit Vancouver. The disease is greed. Greed here is like goitre in Nepal. Everybody's got it so we think we're normal. Greed is a strange illness; other people die because we've got it."

Her finale was dramatic. She said, "The worst crime in the desert is not murder or theft, but knowing where there is water and not telling." She flung her arms wide and said, "So, my friends, I must tell you I have found an oasis in Jesus Christ. Water to wash in. Pure water to drink."

With grace and style Helen had carried the hour, and when it was all over and her friends and family gathered around her, she quietly accepted their congratulations.

Finally James, the ball-playing partner of her childhood days, offered his compliments, paired with the question that was probably in the back of everyone's mind. "Well done, Helen, but—why did you leave your hair standing up on both sides like a scarecrow?"

Helen Huston's convocation address was printed in its entirety in *The New Trail*, the magazine of the university's alumni association. As the lead-in to the story, "By Word and Life: Helen Huston of the UMN," editor Rick Pilger wrote, *"There is something about Helen Huston. Something of the majestic mountains for which Nepal is famous. Something fine and eternal and even a little remote."*

His article concluded, *"And Helen Huston has served them happily. Their land has become a part of her."*

42

Just Like Helen

It was perhaps inevitable that years of never-ending work and sleepless nights, not to mention constant exposure to airborne and water-borne infections, should take their toll.

Helen should have come from her April, 1983, holiday in India refreshed, but she returned to Kathmandu suffering from pleurisy, fever and bronchitis. She took eighteen days of sick-leave and then, still not completely recovered, insisted on returning to Amp Pipal. Normally so strong, she struggled for breath nearly all the way up the hills.

Two months later a severe crampy pain woke her in the middle of the night. When its sharpness wouldn't go away she pounded on the floor to wake the nurses living below. The nurses contacted a recently arrived doctor from Holland and he gave her an injection for the pain.

The next morning, Helen still felt sick and an examination showed signs of internal bleeding. Her co-worker Dr. Margaretta Hook, suspected she needed an urgent operation but felt uneasy about operating on a colleague at Amp Pipal, where facilities for major surgery were limited. She sent a runner to UMN headquarters requesting a helicopter to evacuate her patient to the UMN's larger Patan Hospital.

With all the strength she could muster, Helen resisted, but for once she was overruled. The helicopter pilot dropped down through thick monsoon clouds onto the *maidan* by the hospital. Half an hour later he landed, with Helen aboard, in Kathmandu.

Helen's pain didn't return after her admission, but Patan doctors advised her not to return to the hills. The severe middle-of-the-night pain could easily recur. They felt she was sitting on a time bomb and decided to operate. They found an unusual type of internal hernia, something so rare that one of the doctors took off his operating gloves to pick up a camera and get a colour picture of it. It was just like Helen, they said, to have a condition so unusual that they had to read the fine print in the surgical textbooks just to locate it.

She made a good recovery from the operation but her colleagues began to worry about her health. One of those most worried was Amp Pipal medical director Dr. Del Haug. He said, "I was really concerned over the toll taken on Helen by stress and heavy work. She just gives herself unstintingly. The frequent nights of broken sleep and worrying about people have caused her such fatigue and made her susceptible to illnesses."

Before she left for furlough two years after the operation, Del suggested that when she returned her workload should be lightened to half-time doctor and half-time hospital chaplain. Helen resisted the change. Her two hands could still function as a doctor's hands. Medicine was her life and gave her fulfilment like nothing else could. She wanted to be a full member of the team, not "put on the shelf."

She volunteered to keep an open mind during her furlough. In Canada she wrote exhaustive lists of pros and cons which balanced fairly evenly. But as soon as she arrived at Amp Pipal in January, 1986, she knew what she wanted—to be a full-time doctor again.

She worked as hard as ever at Amp Pipal Hospital before she had another setback. If you talk to her now, she'll deny that it was a heart attack. What it was, well, she's not quite sure, but it definitely was no heart attack.

She had taken the walk uphill from the hospital a thousand times before, but on this night, a month after her return from Canada, a deep-seated pain in her chest seized her and would not go away. This sort of pain brought on by exertion was fairly easy to diagnose; she had suffered a heart attack.

With no electrocardiogram to confirm it, her colleague, Dr. Ian Smith, decided to take no chances. He put Helen to bed in the old mission house on the ridge and managed the feat of keeping her there for five full days, under the care of nurse Marlene Evans. She was then allowed up and around and, at the end of another two weeks, was given permission to walk down to her house. Soon after, she returned to work.

It simply could not have been what they said it was, she decided. Why, only a few days earlier, she had walked almost to the top of Lig Lig Mountain to attend a wedding without any trouble at all. "Very sorry to have frightened everybody," she said.

The weeks of enforced rest reminded her of her own mortality. Was God trying to show her that her fallible flesh was like that of other mortals? If she still wanted to be His servant here, she had better change her ways. She had to acknowledge the signs of wasting and aging.

Even so, the idea of giving up being a full-time doctor was just as dispiriting as ever—"like I just don't count for much any more."

For thirty-five years medical work had "swallowed her up," dominated her life and, as she admitted later, in effect had become her reason for being. She still loved it, but certainly could not perform as she once did, got tired much more easily and found night calls increasingly hard to take.

During the last week of her convalescence, Dr. Mike Haskins, the hospital's surgeon, a fellow Canadian, visited her. He patiently sat listening as she described her dilemma—whether to give up looking after sick people to fill a chaplaincy role that seemed so much less important.

A man of few, well-chosen words, Mike said he could understand her feelings, being asked to take on a new ministry, to comfort the seriously ill and the dying, to relieve anxiety and fear in patients and their families, to pray for their needs and tell them about Jesus' love for them.

Then he asked, "Do you really think that sort of work is less important?" And he quietly added, "I don't think so."

After Mike left, Helen made her decision. She would finish the job she had been asked to do almost twenty years earlier. She would see to it that Amp Pipal really did become the "Hospital of the Living Word."

She had attempted great things for God in the past. But nothing had been done without leaning heavily upon Him. Without His help the hospital would not have been built, not in a thousand years. And she knew Him well enough to expect more great things in the new role she would gladly accept.

43

The Tour Guide

Almost twenty years from opening day, I toured through Amp Pipal Hospital with Helen as my guide. We eased our way through throngs of patients crowded in front of the patient registration area—Tibetans wearing long heavy robes and bright rows of beads, slender, barefoot women breast-feeding their infants, older men wearing topis and leaning for support on sticks.

We ducked into the lab where the technician, Gopal, peered down a microscope in search of TB bacteria, and Lila cross-matched blood specimens.

We passed by the cashier's wicket, where I was surprised to learn that the hospital is still forty-five per cent self-sufficient, even though operating costs and salaries have steadily increased and one in four patients is treated free of charge.

We looked into the pharmacy and said *namaste* to Nil Prasad, a local boy who is now director of that department. Helen showed me the area behind the pharmacy, where intravenous fluids are prepared.

The gateman led us through the gate that opens and closes to control the flow of patients to the examining area, and we met one of the Health Assistants who decides which cases to refer to a doctor. In the office of the young man in charge of TB and leprosy control, we learned that a big part of his job is keeping track of "defaulters" who don't keep up their treatment.

In the treatment room, Krishna Dahal changed a dressing; in X-ray, eighteen-year veteran Hem Raj called for the maintenance man to start the generator to provide power before taking a film; and in central supply, Saraswati rolled bandages for sterilization.

There was much more to this "heroic little hospital" that at one time tried to function without all these trained staff members and relied on a single doctor/administrator. It had been a rocky transition for Helen, from a full-time doctor to a combination doctor/ counselor/ chaplain. The fruit of her labour wasn't as easy to measure; before she had clearly seen how people improved with good medical care.

But if the evidence of benefits were hard for Helen to see, her colleagues immediately recognized the value of her ministry to anxious and fearful people and the hopelessly ill. She seemed to have an uncanny sense, knowing when to be silent and when to speak.

To a middle-aged high caste man, a Brahmin, she read the Bible story of the prodigal son. Near the end of the story, when the father runs out to welcome the rebellious son back home, the man put his head in his hands and wept. He told Helen that his own youngest son had a serious problem with alcohol and he wanted him to come back home and to be a friend with the family again.

Helen asked if he wanted her to pray for his son, and they bowed their heads together to talk with God the Father, who has many wayward sons.

She would not have had the luxury of this kind of time as a full-time doctor. Now daily opportunities to meet the deepest hidden needs of people were presenting themselves.

The surgeon who operated on Pema Gurung found an advanced stomach cancer. It was possible to do a simple by-pass operation but nothing more for the cancer. Pema's husband wanted her to be told the truth, but how could that be done without being cruel? He told

Helen that he had done some reading about Jesus, and he wanted his wife to also understand the Good News.

On Helen's third visit to Pema Gurung, she asked outright what the doctor had found at her operation. Helen explained about the tumor, and said the doctor could not remove it but had created a new passage so that she could eat.

"If the disease is still there, am I going to get worse?" Pema asked.

Yes, she would get worse. But in a few days she would be able to go home for a while, enjoy her family and get to know God better. Then Helen sang for her, the beautiful Nepali hymn "Sara Shristiko Malik" (Lord of All Creation), and they talked about life being a fleeting moment for all of us, but heaven, a place where there is no more pain or suffering.

Pema Gurung and her husband returned to their village and were not heard from again. Helen hoped and prayed "that the dear woman's heart was open to trust the Lord."

It was an important ministry, offering comfort and peace, but Helen felt that her own words were powerless to take away the fear of pain and death. "Only if I allow the Spirit to somehow work through me," she said, "will my fumbling words come alive."

From her chaplain's office, tucked back into the hill, back to back with the outpatient's waiting room, Helen brings good things out of store. She distributes coloured picture books to children who may never have held a book in their hands. She reads a story to children, and sometimes adults, who have never had a book read to them.

She offers a choice of books to the patients. The young people ask for adventure stories. The older people ask for books about God. Some want to learn English as a second language. Some want to learn to read Nepali.

They all look at the bright posters that she puts up in the wards and in the hallways.

Chetu Nath read the poster in his room every day as he lay in his bed, unable to move. It said in Nepali, "The man who comes to me I will never turn away." A handsome teenager, Chetu Nath had been joking with his friends as they carried heavy loads along the footpaths. For a split second he lost his footing and the load had snapped his head back, breaking his neck. Now he was paralyzed, with nowhere to go and nothing to think about—except for that poster on the wall.

Who was that, he asked Helen, who said he wouldn't turn away anyone who came to him? Helen explained that it was Jesus who had made that promise, and then she told him that Jesus loved him and had a wonderful plan for his life. Chetu Nath asked to meet this Jesus, and just as the poster had said, he was welcomed and not turned away.

As genuinely happy and free as Tek Bahadur became after he met this same Jesus, Chetu Nath now lives in the private room that was built for Tek. He helps Helen with the tape and book library and is being tutored in English and Nepali. His face literally lights up when Helen comes to visit, as she often does, not because she feels it her duty, but because "he's an important part of my life."

After several months' work as a chaplain, she had seen enough of God's grace to be able to say, "Maybe the opportunities I have now are every bit as valuable, even though it might seem that my 'medical hands' have been handcuffed. I haven't made the changeover all that well, but I'm grateful for the new work God has given me."

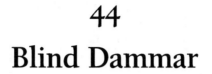

44

Blind Dammar

Dammar, a blind boy about twenty years of age, often tapped his way along the path to Helen's house and sat there in the sun on the verandah. Blind since early childhood from Vitamin A deficiency, he lived with his parents one half hour's walk down the steep hill from the hospital. He spent his hours in idleness.

During the latter part of 1987 Dammar would walk up to the hospital at 7:00 a.m. to meet Helen for a time of reading aloud, singing and praying. He wanted to know about the Lord who long ago restored the sight of the blind.

Saturday mornings they would walk up the rocky path to attend worship service in the Amp Pipal church. Remarkably sensitive to bends and rocks in the path, Dammar walked on in front of Helen, needing only the odd word to keep him on the path. A radar-like sixth sense seemed to guide him.

One day the following March, Dammar prayed aloud for the first time, asking God to keep him from evil and to keep him faithful. It was a very moving moment for Helen.

But there was more to be done. True, he was a simple, illiterate country boy with incurable blindness, but surely there must be a place of usefulness for him somewhere, Helen reasoned.

She made enquiries: Father Tom Gafney, a Jesuit priest living in Kathmandu, could make a place for him in a hostel in a village close to the city. There, along with six other blind men, he could learn rug-weaving, a skill within his capabilities.

Helen visited Dammar a couple of months later. He was slowly learning how to weave but life was lonely. None of the other blind men were Christian. One of them could read Braille and Helen wondered about getting a Braille Bible that could be read to Dammar. About that visit Helen wrote:

"Dammar said, 'please tell my mother and father not to worry about me. . . I am happy here.' We sang a few hymns together; he knows the words and sings well with someone to lead. Good job he couldn't see because tears were streaming down my face as we prayed."

Dammar made progress with rug-weaving, but loneliness and homesickness never left him and he asked to return to his village. With a little help he learned the basics of raising pigs; now he has a small income and much of his time is spent doing useful things.

On one of their walks together, Dammar asked Helen if all the people in Canada knew about God. She answered him honestly, that many people in her country don't believe there is a God.

He looked rather puzzled, "How do they think the world was created?"

Helen said many people think no one created the world, but somehow began long ago with a "big bang."

Dammar stopped walking and started to laugh. Helen found herself laughing with him. With due respect to the supporters of the "big bang" theory, it struck them as funny that the great Creator could be dismissed that easily.

45

Gratitude and Praise

It's hard to get Helen to look back.

She's so completely absorbed and immersed in the present—the immediate pleasures and problems—that it's a struggle to get her to sit down and reflect on the past. She keeps in touch with the times too, listening daily to BBC World News broadcasts and reviews and reading whatever out-of-date magazines find their way into the hills.

The future does not concern her unduly, it is in God's hands, but she is always open to new ideas to make the work of the mission more effective.

If you're lucky enough to persuade her to talk about past days, as I once was, you will find yourself in for a treat. She bubbles over with joy and enthusiasm for people and events long since buried deep in time. But you may have difficulty keeping her on track if you're looking for tales and stories about herself.

In January, 1989 I asked her to share her feelings after nearly thirty-six years as a medical missionary in India and Nepal. Could she sum up in a few words the years of experience since that day in 1953 when she walked the gangplank to board the SS Empress of France?

Her heart overflowed with thankfulness. Nothing—absolutely nothing—could match the overwhelming feeling of gratitude to God for the privilege of being His servant for thirty-six years. Her expressions of gratitude could have filled pages.

First and foremost, she felt grateful to God for having chosen her for "this particular little job in the hills of Nepal." And it was always good to know that "God did not leave me striving to please Him in my own strength."

She could never forget the love and prayers of her parents and other friends. "It's a rare person who can have so many people praying for her; I didn't deserve it."

How could she ever thank the United Church for supporting her work in Asia for thirty-five years? And was there any way to say thank you to the thousands who cared enough about people in the Third World to give gifts for her work?

She was thankful for the priceless gift of education, including all the schooling she needed and the training to become a doctor. Every day she spoke to women who couldn't write their own names.

She appreciated and loved the people of Nepal. There were good and bad among them—as in every nation—but she had found them especially lovable. It was a privilege to live in another culture, learn the language and get close to the people.

She loved the gentle, warm monsoon rains and the sparkling clear October days that followed; she loved the great trees, the flaming red poinsettia bushes, the exquisite hibiscus flowers, the mosses, ferns and orchids growing on the trunks of trees, the funny little green *geko* (salamander) that consumed troublesome bugs in her house. She loved the massive white craggy mountains —"the eternal snows," "the mountains that speak peace to the people."

Worshipping with Nepali Christians filled her with gratitude. They all acknowledged the same Lord and that united them under one banner, although they hardly could have been more different. She shared in their inescapable trials and sorrows and rejoiced when they rejoiced.

It was a privilege to care for sick people and a great joy to see them get better. She was "so thankful for the close relationship that develops when you care for very ill people." But was always bothered when they revered her as if she were a god: "they didn't realize that I'm just an ordinary girl."

It was good to feel needed and to be doing useful work. And it was a priceless privilege to talk to others about the Good News that Jesus brought.

She was full of thanks that she could be a worker in the United Mission to Nepal and for all the missionary colleagues, past and present. So many of them were "caring people." She had learned much from them and many had helped her in her spiritual pilgrimage. Their prayers had sustained her through many a stormy time.

She was thankful that God did not desert her during those stormy times. He did not throw her aside because she wondered to herself, "Is there really a God?" "Is it all make believe?" In fact, at just those times "He always comes and overwhelms me with the assurance that He is and that He rewards those who trust in Him."

Her eyes filled with tears of joy when she spoke of gratitude to God for all her friends. Life was often lonely and few people feel loneliness like the aging unmarried woman.

She could lay claim to a priceless possession that grew not out of blood ties but love, and love alone. Friends like Gesina Janssen who saw her rarely but never forgot Helen's kindness when she arrived as a new intern at the Royal Alex Hospital in 1952; Mia Voreland who spoke of Helen's friendship as "a treasure in my life"; Beth Brunemeier who described her as "my caring, encouraging friend"; Mildred Sullivan whose love and support and weekly letters sustained her through years of trials and joys.

The list could go on. She had friends all across Canada and in many countries around the world. God had endowed her with bountiful blessings, almost too numerous to count, that filled her heart to overflowing with thankfulness. But the jewel of all those enduring friendships sparkled as the most cherished gift of all.

*****

Has Helen changed much over the years? Tata talks about her hair being streaked with silver, and then goes on to say "that increases her value."

The stooped shoulders of aging have changed the contours of her once ramrod-straight back. At one time the hike up from Palangtar was for her little more than a stroll in the park; in 1984 she described it: "A blistering hot walk. Lay in the shade many times. Took seven hours to do what I have done in four."

Signs of outward aging could not be denied, but most of her friends and associates believed that "the inner person" had not aged one bit and, if anything, had matured and grown more beautiful.

In 1987 Jay and Ruth Story wrote of Helen's faithfulness over the years since 1954 in Allahabad and how her life is "a marvellous story of the grace of God revealed in one earthen vessel." Tata said her *didi* (older sister) is the same as she has always been and for that "I am very thankful to God."

Helen's supreme goal has remained unaltered: that everyone should know God and the forgiveness and love of Jesus Christ. When a patient or relative expressed a desire to know the Truth, she would bend heaven and earth to show them the Way.

Hers was a life of prayer. Her letters were often full of prayer requests: "Pray for B.K., the paraplegic. Remember K. who is living in a hostile environment in his village. Lord, please remember T. and M.M. and make them an instrument of Your peace."

Her prayers came as easily and naturally as breathing. Someone said that she prayed "as if Jesus were there in the room." She prayed openly and unashamedly. Sometimes her prayers were full of praise and thanksgiving; at other times she agonized over the needs and sorrows of others or her own human fallibility.

Prayer was the spring and strength of her life. Without it she never would have survived the responsibility of Dhar hospital, the horrors of the cholera epidemic, the staggering demands of the dispensary and the turmoil of the strike.

Her day began with prayer, and often at 4:00 a.m., well before the sun touched the spiny crags of the Himalayas, and ended in the same way. Bowing her head in the presence of the Lord conferred upon her a strength, a peace and a mysterious freedom and poise.

229

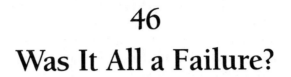

46

Was It All a Failure?

Thirty-two years of Helen's life had been devoted to the people of the hilly Gorkha District of Nepal; she and many others like Nora Vickers, Howard Barclay and Asbjorn Voreland had made invaluable contributions.

Had anything of value been accomplished? Had Helen lived to see the realization of her own hopes and aspirations, the fruits of her years of labour?

In many ways, there was little cause to rejoice.

She had prayed much and worked hard to make it a "Hospital of the Living Word," and so many things pointed to failure. In fact, in all honesty, could anyone call it a Christian hospital? In 1984, when evil men clutched the hospital staff in their grip, none of the Christians opposed them.

And just how many of the Nepali staff were Christian? In the early days after 1969, staff and missionaries were like a family and "we all gathered together at 10:00 a.m. for morning prayers," as Annama related. By 1987 the staff numbered seventy-six Hindu and four Christians. In 1989 the number of Christians was down to two.

The impact of the mission on the community disappointed many. For over thirty-one years the UMN had offered a variety of fine services, carefully seeking approval of the local *panchayat* as they went along and respecting the wishes of the people.

Had the villagers done anything on their own initiative? Or had they developed a "handout mentality," content to do little and wait around for more to be doled out? They certainly liked the convenience of the hospital, but some skeptical missionaries doubted if many people really cared about the health of their own community.

What about the church in Nepal? It's doubtful Helen had missed many days in praying for it, often earnestly, passionately. Had the Amp Pipal church been a strong, thriving and faithful group of believers, Helen could have accepted other hurts and failures.

Sadly, the small, weak church seemed unable to grow beyond infancy. Lacking effective leadership and consistent support, it commanded little respect from the community. Bickerings and disputes often ended with harsh words. During one meeting, a young man took great offence because the current version of the Nepali New Testament "was not the Word of God." When Tom Hale pointed out that it was a faithful translation, adapted to make it easier to understand, the man walked out and never came back.

The congregation from the village of Lamagara, about five hours' walk away, could hardly have been more different. The villagers, all members of the Tamang ethnic group, were nearly all Christian and many of them had paid a price for their faith. One day in 1987 Helen attended a service there, over 250 had jammed into the building. Many of the people could not read one word of the Bible. They asked Helen—not for handouts—but for teachers so they might learn about the Bible and about good health.

Her own family caused her heartache and grief. She constantly prayed for them. In 1973 she sent a tape home with a message for each member of the family and their children, expressing her concern for their salvation and the hope that "in a hundred years we could all gather around the throne of grace." Not everyone appreciated the message; in fact, some of them resented it.

Each day she was conscious of her own failings and fraility. She longed to be worthy of the name of Christ. "Create in me a clean heart, O God," was often on her lips. Yet there was a never-ending battle within. To her friend Mildred she wrote:

"Please know I need your help. . . I feel so vulnerable and incapable this morning (and often) but I can sure do a quick switch—alas. Couple of temper outbursts—somehow one thinks one has got that licked—then Boom!"

Like the apostle Paul, she was embattled, but never in despair. Her head was "bloody, but unbowed." It often seemed that she was losing out on all fronts, but there was one consolation. Jesus too had been defeated, completely and utterly.

For Helen, disappointments and failings were there, to be sure, but over and above them rose a mountain of things for which she could rejoice and give thanks, a mountain like Himal Chuli that soared into the Asian sky.

True, it was not yet the Hospital of the Living Word that Helen had envisaged, but in another sense it was just that.

Under that corrugated aluminum roof doctors, nurses, cleaners and clerks, all had some understanding of Christian principles and standards and were motivated to apply them in their daily duties.

And patients coming from far and wide knew there was something different about the hospital, and to get to it they willingly took long bus rides, walked or were carried for up to eight days. They accepted the fact of a spiritual element to the ministry with prayer as part of it. Many felt safe in the Christian hospital, safe from the pervasive power of witches and evil spirits.

If most of the Nepali staff stood aloof, unwilling to commit themselves to becoming Christians, it was because they lived in fear, fear of the terrible consequences.

They knew only too well that Hindu society treated the despised Christians like traitors. Around Amp Pipal the predominant Brahmin caste, like the rigid Pharisees of old, dealt harshly with those who departed from Hindu orthodoxy.

With the heating-up of the government's campaign against

Christians, why should the hospital employees risk beatings and jailings? And how could they be proper citizens of Nepal with the prevailing view that anyone worshipping Christ was "unpatriotic?"

Government restrictions against any form of proselytizing were well known. An official visited Amp Pipal Hospital in 1986, and issued a stern warning. The custom of touring through the wards singing carols on Christmas Eve had to be abandoned in 1989.

Only God knew how many of the hospital staff lived their lives and did their daily work as "silent believers." Perhaps it would take more than government edicts and social disapproval to stamp out the Good News.

If at times the Amp Pipal community expressed indifference or even hostility to the mission, thousands of individuals felt otherwise.

Both Shobba and Iman had held responsible jobs in the hospital over the years and had seen the ravages of tuberculosis, hookworm amenia, malnutrition and diarrhea in children; they expressed their views in simple terms—"the hospital has done much for the community."

Iman went beyond that:

"Before the mission came, it was impossible for ordinary village boys and girls to get any kind of education. Now, many of these same children have taken positions of responsibility all over the country—on the university campuses, in business and industry and in government."

If Iman's assessment was correct, then the mission's achievement was a remarkable one.

And indeed "Gorkha graduates" stood out like beacons all over the country.

Skinny little Dil Bahadur took on the job of overseer of the entire crew building a dam for the huge Andhi Khola Hydroelectric Project; young Jiwan became a political leader in the Gorkha District; Krishna Rana progressed to become Principal of the Nepali Language School in Kathmandu.

Yagya Karki completed university and then took his Ph.D. training in Britain and a subsequent executive job with an international development agency; young Dak Gurung studied agriculture in Canada before returning to Kathmandu where he established his own market garden and later "The Gorkha Restaurant."

Upendra Devkota went on to study medicine after finishing school at the UMN school not far from Amp Pipal. He travelled to Britain for specialty training in neurosurgery and eventually joined the staff of Kathmandu's Teaching Hospital where he gained a reputation for professional excellence.

Only a few became Christian but all of them learned something of Christian principles and virtues.

That a church in any form existed in Amp Pipal had to be considered a miracle; on all sides hostile forces seemed bent on destroying it.

Especially in the villages, where people lived lives so dependent on one another, a "deserter" from the Hindu fold could expect to be greeted: "We'll cut you off. We'll not help you in the fields. We'll not come to your house or eat with you or even drink water from a container you have touched."

Weak in numbers at any given time, the Amp Pipal church would have teemed with committed believers had they all been able to assemble together. But like the village boys and girls seeking education, Christians too had left the meagre pickings in the hills for opportunity elsewhere.

The seed had been sown in their hearts during their formative years and many of them, after leaving behind the restrictions of the village, blossomed as mature Christians.

Carl Friedricks once said, "Some of the finest Christians in Nepal have come from the Gorkha District."

But if the church was small in number, it could hardly be described as weak. In fact, one day Tata made her point very clearly, asserting boldly in her own language the English equivalent of "Don't you dare call us weak!"

She was, of course, right: within the ranks of the *mandali* (congregation) there stood erect a number of stalwart, faithful believers. Most had put up with hardship and humiliation for their faith, yet they rejoiced and remained loyal to the Lord.

Helen loved the little church at Amp Pipal, rejoiced to see evidence of spiritual growth and maturity and warmly welcomed new believers. But her role was that of a supporter and encourager, not a leader. The church had no pastor; those who could teach from the Bible did so, and Helen took her turn.

But she believed the church had to be indigenous and not stamped with the imprint of any Western country or culture. It must be the church of those who lived in those green hills.

Amp Pipal would never become another Lamagara where almost everyone in the village had thrown away their idols to worship Jesus.

Helen believed that one faithful disciple is worth a hundred shallow believers and Amp Pipal could claim the sort of people worthy to be called "bright gems for His crown."

The Amp Pipal Hospital complex.

47

Finishing the Course

I have fought a good fight.
I have finished my course.
I have kept the faith.
2 Timothy 4:7

She turned away from the rough wooden lectern and joined us, sitting cross-legged on a straw mat on the floor. Her scarlet blouse was a perfect match for the red poinsettias that decorated the church on this morning in 1988, a week before Christmas. It was an unusually grey and dreary day in Amp Pipal, but warmth and light seemed to fill the small stone structure from its open rafters to the mud floor.

I studied the stately figure of Dr. Helen Huston, my colleague and friend, on her turn to address the Amp Pipal Christian family. In this place where quietness rises as the mist from the valley floor and where giant poinsettias grow wild, she had poured out the years of her life and now she poured out joy.

There were only twenty-six in our group of Christians that morning, but she spoke in Nepali as though she were addressing an audience of thousands. Quietly and confidently, she paused every few minutes to give a brief translation in English to help the handful of Westerners not fluent in Nepali.

Her Christmas message that morning was delivered with pure, irrepressible joy and her face positively shone with a luminous glow. It was impossible not to be swept into her enthusiasm as she opened her arms wide as though to embrace the entire group. She described the height and breadth and depth of love that planned and carried out "the greatest event in human history."

Sparkling blue eyes scanned the room to meet the eyes of everyone in the circle. She spoke of the day when "the Creator of the universe became a human, a human like each of us," and then, as if perplexed, she knit her brow. "Why would He choose to come as a lowly child, born in a barn for farm animals?" Many of her listeners owned a cow or a few goats, or maybe even a water buffalo.

We listened as she talked of the world's black shadows and tragedies. On that same December morning, Armenian people were recovering from a devastating earthquake. In nearby Bangladesh, floods were wiping out villages and precious rice fields. Closer to home, in Amp Pipal Hospital just before dawn, a child had died.

So many people endure such suffering and hardship. Why pretend that it is otherwise? But Jesus gives hope to the sufferer and He fills with compassion the hearts of others to help them in their distress.

Her message that day was joy—pure, unmitigated, free flowing, irrepressible and life-giving. There was barely contained excitement in her voice and youthful enthusiasm in her manner, although fine wrinkles and lines creased her face, and her long hair, braided and pinned up at the back, was tinged with grey.

I felt moved by the warmth, sincerity and conviction of her words— an expression of her deepest and strongest beliefs, of the guiding principles of her entire life. Nothing could have been more real; the love of Jesus Christ was by far the most important thing. Her faith in Him permeated all.

I heard her voice, but I found myself staring down at the red mud floor, looking back in time, seeing beyond the wrinkles, the tired eyes, the silver hair.

Was this the same girl who had shouted at God during a blustering thunderstorm at Sylvan Lake? It certainly was the tall, bright-eyed medical student whose exuberant laughter I had heard rippling through the anatomy lab. I thought about the young woman standing by the ship's rail, with tears in her eyes, as she sailed out of Montreal harbour in 1953. And tears of a different kind when she bowed her head under a great flowering tree at Allahabad, asked God's forgiveness and committed her life to Jesus.

I thought about Dhar Hospital in India, and her first exposure to tuberculosis and leprosy, and Hat Piplia, where eight of her frail patients died in one week in spite of her fervent prayers.

I could never forget her talking about the 1960 visit to Amp Pipal, and her first sighting of the eternal snows of Mt. Himal Chuli and Manaslu. I was filled with admiration, for those amazing years when she and Nora and Becky and others worked such long hours in the little dispensary, only a few hundred metres down the hill from the church where we were sitting.

I marvelled at the unbelievable achievement of planning and building a hospital up the the high hills many miles from any road.

In my mind's eye I could see her, needle in hand, rushing to start the intravenous fluids that alone could save the lives of cholera victims in the teeming refugee camps of West Bengal. This same hand would remove her mortarboard to allow Dr. Amy Zelmer to drape over her shoulders the mantle of the Honorary Doctor of Laws at the University of Alberta.

I thought of her gradually relinquishing her pioneering, leadership role to others, and then giving up most of her beloved medical work after her illness of January, 1986. I thought of all the grief and heartache she had endured when her own staff showed themselves to be dishonest and rebellious.

I thought of the lingering disappointment she must have felt—"the Hospital of the Living Word" had never become a reality, far from it.

I saw her, an aging, single lady missionary spending her last term in her beloved Nepal and starting now to think about "going home" to Canada when there was really no home to go to. I could not deny a feeling of sadness; she had given of herself completely and unreservedly for thirty-six years and now the end was not far off.

I was conscious of a silence and lifted by gaze from the mud floor to her face. The feeling of sadness was mine, not hers. I joined in her joy and realized there was no reason to feel sorry for Helen Huston. Before me was a person whose life has been amazingly purposeful and filled with inexpressible freedom. She sat before us all, rejoicing. She had rejoiced all her life, and would continue to do so.

48

The Greatest Need

It was the first-ever press conference to be called on the grounds of the United Mission to Nepal headquarters in Kathmandu.

Just back from Canada where she had received the Hillary Award for Humanitarian Service, Helen Huston stood beside a tall tree to address a battery of reporters and photographers, seated on chairs in the garden. The date was December 13, 1991.

The sun shone on the gathering as they asked about her feelings after getting the prestigious award.

"It came completely out of the blue!" she said. "I didn't even know there was such a thing as a Sir Edmund Hillary Foundation. . . . They had somehow heard of me and wrote a letter. They gave me the award on November 21 . . . and it was a good opportunity for me to find out more about the great work Sir Hillary has been doing."

The reporters wanted to know why she had come to Nepal in the first place and if she thought the quality of life had improved for village people in the past thirty years. They wanted specifics about her work with emotionally disturbed patients and those suffering from leprosy. They asked about her work to improve the status of women in Nepal.

Then one reporter asked a question which gave Dr. Huston of Nepal an opportunity to sum up the centre and the focus of her life. In the country which still has massive needs, she was asked, "What is Nepal's greatest need?"

Half-smiling, half-nodding, she pondered only a moment before offering her reply to this probing question. It came quietly and confidently. "Nepal's greatest need is the same as Canada's. What our countries need, more than anything else, are men and women with new hearts."

Dr. Helen Huston responding to reporters.

Historical Note

Many people consider the birth and growth of the United Mission to Nepal nothing short of a miracle.

The first facet of the miracle was that Christian missionaries were even allowed into Nepal in the first place. The government was suspicious of all foreigners, but hostile to Christians.

Curiously enough, the UMN owed its origins in part to those delightful feathered creatures that chirp and warble in the treetops of Nepal.

In 1949, a biologist named Dr. Bob Fleming taught science at a school in northern India. Some of his students were children of diplomats and missionaries. His wife, Dr. Bethel Fleming, served as a medical doctor at the nearly Landour Community Hospital. Both were supported by the American Methodist Board.

Bob Fleming loved birds and had taken part in several expeditions in India to collect specimens for the Chicago Natural History Museum. He grew more and more intrigued by what he heard about the variety of unique species of birds in Nepal and applied for government permission to visit the tightly-closed country.

Surprised that his request was granted, he set off on foot in October, 1949, for a three-month expedition. In his party was a medical missionary from central India, Dr. Carl Taylor, who was able to take a leave from work because Bethel Fleming agreed to replace him. He carried basic medical supplies with him.

The three months proved to be a highly successful pioneering expedition for Fleming, who retrieved specimens from 256 species of birds. But Dr. Taylor returned aghast, for he had never before seen so much sickness and disease, and much of it treatable. Fleming had seen the disease too and was determined to return to Nepal.

A few years later he did go back, this time with Bethel and their two children, as well as another medical doctor, Dr. Carl Friedericks and his family. Carl and Betty Friedericks were missionaries sent to India by the American Presbyterians.

This time the doctors would stay for six weeks, setting up clinics in Tansen, a large town in the hills thirty-two kilometres from the Indian border. At the end of six weeks of hard work, they felt as if they had dropped out of a marathon after fifteen minutes of running. So much of the medical work remained untouched.

The people of Tansen felt deeply thankful for the medical help to their community, thanked the missionaries for coming and formally requested them to return to establish a hospital in Tansen.

That request weighed heavily upon them, but they did not have permission to work permanently in Nepal. From India, they let their mission boards know about the need and their willingness to go, and they prayed for an open door. Finally, in early 1952, they wrote to the Prime Minister of Nepal asking for permission to open a permanent medical work at Tansen.

On furlough in the United Sates, the Friedericks were given the go-ahead to raise money for a proposed Tansen Hospital, and support was given by the Presbyterian Board to help form a mission to Nepal, provided it was interdenominational.

In January, 1953, the Flemings visited Kathmandu, where Bethel inspected the few existing health care facilities. They wrote a second letter to the Prime Minister, asking again for permission to start a medical work in Tansen, and offering to set up material and child welfare clinics in the Kathmandu Valley.

On May 18, 1953, the Ministry of Foreign Affairs gave permission for both projects. Although reasons for the breakthrough were never given, it may ultimately have had something to do with the royal family. Crown Prince Mahendra had just lost his wife in childbirth with their sixth child.

Mission representatives in India lost no time. The Presbyterian and Methodist Boards brought together other church missions and societies to plan an international and interdenominational mission for Nepal. Bob and Bethel Fleming were appointed the first American Methodist missionaries to the Himalayan kingdom.

Drs. Bethel and Bob Fleming, pioneer founders of the UMN.

At a meeting in Nagpur, India in March, 1954, the United Mission to Nepal was born. By the following September, eight churches and missionary bodies were accepted as charter members.

The locked doors of Nepal were open. From the outset, the government made it clear that promoting Christianity would not be tolerated. The government also insisted that the mission bear all costs, charge no fees to patients, train and hire Nepalis whenever possible, and be prepared to eventually turn everything over to the government.

After 35 years of work under the conditions set by the government, the UMN grew to include 392 missionaries working in education, rural development, engineering and industrial development and health care. Workers from 18 countries served with the UMN under the sponsorship of 37 church and missionary societies.

The present executive director of the UMN, Edgar Metzler, was recently asked by a Nepali government official who had observed Christian agencies at work in development and disaster relief, "Where do these people get the sense of duty to do such social service?"

Metzler replied that the service was not given from a sense of duty but out of gratitude. They have all experienced the love and grace of God, and sharing through service was their expression of thanks to God.

The author and his wife spent twelve of the best years of their lives in Nepal with the UMN. For these "best years," they have Helen Huston to thank. Dr. Gerry Hankins was called to replace her for a short period at Amp Pipal Hospital in 1970, and there he found that he could also make "some sort of a contribution." Just as important, he and his wife discovered that missionaries were remarkably warm and friendly people, and they would be happy to belong to their ranks.

With their daughter Jennifer, they returned to Nepal on a long-term basis in 1974, to work at the larger Shanta Bhawan Hospital in Kathmandu. Their contacts with Helen Huston were intermittent, but they grew to love this tall vibrant woman and soon found out that, as a pioneering missionary-doctor, she had acquired the stature of a legendary figure within the UMN.